Babe Ruth and Hank Aaron
The Home Run Kings

The young Babe Ruth. *(Private collection)*

Hank Aaron when he was with the Milwaukee Braves.
(Milwaukee Braves)

Babe Ruth and Hank Aaron
The Home Run Kings

by James Haskins

ILLUSTRATED WITH PHOTOGRAPHS

LOTHROP, LEE & SHEPARD COMPANY
NEW YORK

By James Haskins

Babe Ruth and Hank Aaron: *The Home Run Kings*
From Lew Alcindor to Kareem Abdul Jabbar

Jacket photographs courtesy of the New York Yankees and the Atlanta Braves.

Printed in the United States of America.

1   2   3   4   5   78   77   76   75   74

Library of Congress Cataloging in Publication Data

Haskins, James (date)
  Babe Ruth and Hank Aaron; the home run kings.

  SUMMARY: A dual biography of Babe Ruth and Hank Aaron, from childhood to championship. Includes comparative statistics, batting averages, and famous games.
  1. Ruth, George Herman, 1895–1948. 2. Aaron, Henry, 1934– . 3. Batting (Baseball).
  [1. Ruth, George Herman, 1895–1948. 2. Aaron, Henry, 1934– . 3. Baseball—Biography] I. Title.
GV865.R8H37   796.357′092′2 [B] [920]   74-11018
ISBN 0-688-41654-3
ISBN 0-688-51654-8 (lib. bdg.)

ACKNOWLEDGMENTS

Grateful acknowledgment is due to Henry Aaron and Mr. and Mrs. Herbert Aaron for their permission to use certain quoted material in this book. Much of the background material on Babe Ruth is from the book *The Babe Ruth Story As Told to Bob Considine*. Copyright, 1948, by George Herman Ruth. Published by E. P. Dutton & Co. and used with their permission. Additional material on Henry Aaron is quoted from "Hank Aaron," by Herbert Nipson, reprinted by permission of *Ebony* Magazine, copyright 1973 by Johnson Publishing Company, Inc., and from The New York Times, © 1974 by The New York Times Company. Reprinted by permission.

Thanks also to Ann Kalkhoff and Carol Politis for their help in gathering material for the book, and to Mary Ellen Arrington, who typed the manuscript. A special thanks to Kathy Benson, without whom this book would not have been possible.

Contents

When Babe Ruth was seven years old he was put into St. Mary's Industrial School in Baltimore

1/
George and Henry:
Growing Up

"I was a bad kid," Babe Ruth used to tell people. "I say that without pride, but with a feeling that it is better to say it. Because I live with one great hope in mind: to help kids who now stand where I stood as a boy."

The Babe did not want other kids to make the same mistakes he had. But he used to admit that it would be pretty hard for a kid not to make mistakes if he had to grow up in the same way he had.

Babe Ruth was born George Herman Ruth, Jr., in Baltimore, Maryland, on February 6, 1895. That was eighty years ago. Most kids today do not even have grandparents who are eighty years old. But even if their grandparents are only fifty or sixty or seventy years old, they remember the great Babe Ruth. And they remember that he rose to fame from a childhood of poverty and much unhappiness.

George Herman Ruth was not born in a hospital. His family was too poor to afford hospital bills, so George was born in the row house at 426 West Camden Street, near Baltimore's waterfront, where his family lived.

It has been written that Babe Ruth was an orphan. He was not. He had both a mother, Kate Schanberg Ruth, and a father, George Herman Ruth, Sr. It's just that they were never around much to be real parents to him.

On the ground floor of the house was Mr. Ruth's saloon. Babe's parents worked twenty hours a day to try to make a living from the business. That left their three children alone to take care of themselves. George was the youngest, but his brother, John, died before he had a chance to be much of a big brother to George. And his sister, Mayme, did not have much control over the little boy.

Often, Mayme could not even find George. As soon as he could walk he began to go downstairs to the saloon, where he listened to the rough talk of the longshoremen, merchant sailors, and waterfront bums who drank there. By the age of five he probably knew more curse words than most twenty-year-olds, and he started chewing tobacco at the age of seven.

When he was not in the saloon, George was out on the neighborhood streets. He got into fights with older and younger boys; he threw rocks at passing horse-drawn buggies; he hung around the shipyards and docks and got into just about every kind of mischief possible.

"I hardly knew my parents," Babe Ruth said many years later. Perhaps that is why he refused to obey them. They had no more control over him than Mayme had. When they told him to stay upstairs, he went right downstairs to the saloon or out onto the streets. "Looking back on my early childhood," he later said, "I honestly don't remember being aware of the difference between right and wrong. If my parents had something that I wanted very badly, I took it, but I must have had some dim realization that this was stealing because it never occurred to me to take the property of anyone besides my immediate family."

George's parents did not see the difference. He stole, he swore, he chewed tobacco, he stayed out late and he would not mind. They had to work too hard in the saloon to take care of him properly, they decided. On June 13, 1902, when George was seven, his parents placed him in St. Mary's Industrial School in Baltimore.

St. Mary's was an orphanage, a reform school and a training school all in one. It took in boys who were homeless, who were unwanted, who were runaways, or who were delinquents and tried to give them an education and training in some skill. When George entered, he was listed as an "incorrigible," which means a child who cannot be corrected, who cannot be made to obey.

The people at St. Mary's were good people. They cared about the boys and they tried to make them feel wanted and at home. If George had been able to stay there without interruption, it would probably have proved a good, stable home for him. But he was not even allowed that. Entering St. Mary's in June 1902, he was released to his parents in July 1902. Kate and

George Ruth, Sr., were good people too, and they felt bad about sending their son away. They had missed him and decided to try again. George would not mind his parents any better after a month at St. Mary's than before. In November, he was sent back to the school.

His parents moved to a new neighborhood in December. It was a better neighborhood than West Camden Street, and once again they thought maybe they could succeed with their son. George was again released to them, and he stayed for two years. But in 1904, when he was nine, he was sent back.

And so it went. From 1904 to 1908 George was at St. Mary's. In 1908, when he was thirteen, he returned home, but then his mother died. His father did not feel he could take care of his son alone; he sent George back to St. Mary's. George was back home again in 1911, back at St. Mary's in 1912. With all his "entered" and "released" dates, George's record was longer than that of any other boy in the school.

If Hank Aaron had been born one day later than he was, he would have shared birthdays with the man with whom he would one day share the home run record. As it was, Henry Aaron was born on February 5, 1934, just one day before Babe Ruth's thirty-ninth birthday and in the year of Ruth's twenty-third and next to last regular baseball season. Thus, Henry Aaron never got to see Babe Ruth play, and he would not even hear the name Babe Ruth for many years.

Like George Ruth, Henry Aaron was born at home. The Aaron family was poor, like the Ruth family, but that was not the main reason Stella Aaron had all her children at home. The main reason was that, in 1934, southern hospitals did not admit blacks. The hospitals in Mobile, Alabama, where the Aarons lived, were no exception.

Henry Aaron (he was not given a middle name at birth) was born during the height of the Depression. People everywhere in America were having a hard time making ends meet, but for black people it was an especially difficult time. Herbert and Stella Pritchard Aaron were hard-working people. Both had grown up picking cotton and doing chores around their parents' farms. But being willing to work was often not enough in the Depression, when prices were high and jobs were scarce. Herbert Aaron was luckier than many other blacks in the South at that time—he had a job with the Alabama Drydock and Shipbuilding Company as a boilermaker's helper. But his salary barely covered the needs of his family, which, with Henry's birth, numbered five.

"First came Herbert junior," says Mrs. Herbert Aaron, a plump, jovial woman, "then Sarah, and then after Sarah came Henry. We were living in a little two-room apartment, and with a baby and two other little ones running around, well, sometimes it was hard to go from place to place."

There would be more children. About four and a half years after Henry's birth, Tommie would be born, and after him, Alfreda and James. The walls of the little apartment would fairly bulge. The family moved to a rented house on Edwards Avenue in Toulminville, a suburb of Mobile.

The four-and-a-half-year period between the time he was born and the time his younger brother Tommie arrived is the reason Hank Aaron gives when he states that he was "a mama's boy."

"I was the youngest, by more than four years," he says, "and that means Mama had more time for me, when I was little, than she had had for the others. I was too young to play with the older kids anyway, so I stayed around the house a lot. Mama never had to worry."

Hank's mother agrees pretty much with her son's description of himself as a child: "If all children were as easy to raise as Henry was, a lot of mothers would have fewer gray hairs.

"He was my baby until Tommie came along," she goes on. "I had more time for him than I did for the others, I guess. But he wasn't any sissy. He got into his share of mischief, and he sure got his share of lickings."

When asked which of the lickings that Henry received they remember best, both Hank and his mother are in agreement. It was the golf course licking.

Not far from Edwards Avenue was Mobile's municipal golf course. Many of the boys in nearby neighborhoods made good money as caddies there, but Stella Aaron refused to allow her son to set foot on the course.

"I'd never heard of any golf player who wasn't a no-account and a gambler," she says. "Besides, a creek ran through that golf course. I've always been afraid of water, and I kept my children away from it."

That was no easy task, considering the number of creeks, bayous, rivers, and bays of the Gulf Coast town.

But Henry would go to the golf course anyway, and with his friend Cornelius Giles he would hunt golf balls and sell them to the golfers. One day, in their search for golf balls, the two started to cross the creek on some logs that lay across the water. Henry stepped out on them first. They began to roll and slip and Henry lost his balance and fell into the water.

He surfaced, gasping for breath and screaming for help. He couldn't swim! He was sure he would drown, and he probably would have if Cornelius had not jumped in and dragged him out of the water.

Once safe on land, Henry forgot that he had almost drowned and began to worry about his mother. He waited around until his clothes dried before he returned home. But there was one thing he could not hide, and his mother noticed it.

"I had been looking for him and calling for him for I don't know how long, maybe an hour," Stella Aaron recalls. "When he finally came home I was so glad to see him I didn't even think to ask where he'd been. But then I saw him shaking his head and holding his hands over his ears.

"Where you been, boy?" I said to him. "You know your ears don't ache unless you've been in water, and it's too cold for swimming. You've been to that golf course again!"

Hank Aaron still shudders when he remembers what happened next: "For a few minutes after the news came out, I felt that I'd have been better off if I had drowned. She gave me the licking of a lifetime, so bad that I still remember it."

Henry Aaron was a quiet child. "He liked to stay in and read comic books," his mother says. "Later, it was sports books. He liked to be my himself. He had his friends, but he didn't go out and get into a lot of mischief like boys do when they run with a whole group."

All the Aaron children stayed home a lot, for there were many chores for them to do around the house. According to Mrs. Aaron, however, Henry was never very good about doing his share of them. "Henry never did know too much about work," she says.

It has been written that Hank Aaron developed his powerful wrists when he worked hauling ice as a youngster. "That job lasted about two weeks," Mrs. Aaron recalls, "and it was the only job he ever had."

Hank readily agrees with his mother about his attitude toward work. He tells about how he would visit his father's father, Granddaddy Aaron, on the farm where his father grew up. Sometimes he was allowed to stay for several days. He enjoyed the visits until one day his grandfather asked him to help out in the fields. He did not prove to be much of a field hand. "Thank God for baseball, or I might have starved to death," Hank says.

Hank Aaron spent a comfortable childhood. The family was poor but never destitute. His parents were strict, but they cared. He never knew the kind of loneliness that George Ruth did.

George Herman Ruth showed skill in sports very early. While he was still at home with his parents in the apartment above the saloon, George had tagged along with the older boys in the neighborhood. He learned to swim when they threw him into the Patapsco River, the wide feeder into Chesapeake Bay. He learned to play catch by standing outside the older boys' circle and running in front of them to catch the burlap bag full of stones and sand that was their "ball." Even though he received a kick or a bop on the head each time he managed to intercept the bag, George was determined to show the older boys that he was good enough to be included in their games.

At St. Mary's his interest in sports was encouraged. Games were regarded as an important way to help the boys learn to get along with others and to learn good sportsmanship. Every day, except when it rained, George and the others played in the big yard next to the school. They played catch and volleyball, field hockey and baseball. Their equipment was not very good. St. Mary's did not have much money for sports equipment and had to depend on donations of money and balls and bats.

The boys at St. Mary's had an athletics instructor, at least. His name was Brother Matthias, and when he was not teaching classes inside the school he was outside, teaching sports and organizing teams. He proved to be the most important man in George's life, the father he had never really known.

"I don't know why," Babe Ruth would later recall, "but he singled me out when I first came to St. Mary's. It wasn't that I was his 'pet.' But he concentrated on me, probably because I needed it. . . . Brother Matthias saw very early that I had some talent for catching and throwing a baseball. He used to back me into a corner of the big yard at St. Mary's and bunt a ball to me by the hour, correcting the mistakes I made with my hands and feet. . . . I think I was born as a hitter the first day I ever saw him hit a baseball. I can remember it as if it were yesterday."

It was during George's first month at St. Mary's, when he was seven years old. Brother Matthias had decided the boys needed some fielding practice. He went to the end of the yard, a finger mitt on his left hand, a bat in his right. He tossed the ball up in the air with his left hand and gave it a belt with the bat he held in his right hand. The ball went sailing across the yard, clearing the fence in center field about 350 feet away. It was a terrific hit.

Three hundred and fifty feet might not seem like a great distance today, but in 1902 it was a long distance to hit a baseball. Baseballs in those days were not the small, hard, round balls we know. "The baseball of that time was a lump of mush," Babe Ruth later said, "and by the time St. Mary's got hold of one it was considerably less." Not only was the ball a lifeless lump, but

Brother Matthias had hit it that long distance with one hand!

George stood there and could not believe his eyes. He decided that the sight of Brother Matthias, tall and graceful, making the ball soar into the air, was the most beautiful thing he had ever seen in his life. He wanted to learn to hit as well and as gracefully as Brother Matthias.

Coached by Brother Matthias, George worked at his baseball skills. While he had a natural talent, baseball did not come as easily to him as many people think. Every day he practiced. During his periods at home, he practiced with boys in the neighborhood, or by himself. Every time he returned to St. Mary's the boys on his team cheered, for he was a great asset. When he was nine he was playing with the twelve-year-olds. At age twelve he was with the sixteen-year-olds. By the time he was sixteen he was playing with the best teams in the school.

Until George was fourteen or fifteen he preferred to play as catcher. But he was left-handed, and Brother Matthias and many of the older boys insisted that a left-hander could never be a good catcher. Even so, George felt most comfortable in that position.

"We had no catcher's mitt built for left-handers, of course," Babe would later recall. "We were lucky to have any kind of mitt. I'd use the regular catcher's mitt on my left hand, receive the throw from the pitcher, take off the glove and throw it back to him left-handed.

When I had to throw to a base, trying to catch a runner, I'd toss the glove away, grab the ball with my left hand and heave it with everything I had."

Brother Matthias would move George around on the field, in both infield and outfield, but George was best at catcher, and that is the position he played most until he discovered pitching. His pitching debut came about by accident.

He was fourteen or fifteen and his team was being creamed, not because they were making bad plays or hitting poorly, but because their pitchers were giving up hits right and left. One pitcher was tried, then another, then another, until finally George couldn't help laughing. The situation was so hopeless it was funny. He laughed so hard, he doubled up and rolled on the ground. Brother Matthias walked over and asked him what was so funny. When George told him why he was laughing, Brother Matthias suggested that George show everyone how to pitch right.

George stopped laughing. He had never pitched before in his life. He did not know the first thing about it. But he knew he did not have much say in the matter. Looking about him, daring his teammates to laugh at *him*, he walked slowly to the mound. "I am never going to laugh at anyone else again," he promised himself.

Yet, when he reached the pitcher's mound, something happened. He would later remember, "I felt, somehow, as if I had been born out there and that this was a kind of home for me. It seemed the most natural

thing in the world to start pitching—and to start striking out batters. I even tried a curve or two, and, kid-
like, curled my tongue to the corner of my mouth while
doing it."

From that time on, George Ruth was a pitcher.

Henry Aaron also showed skill in sports very early,
and showed an interest in baseball even earlier. The-
odore Blunt, a black policeman who works at Mobile's
airport, was one of the many young men who used to
play baseball on weekends on what they called Council Field, an empty lot across from Council Elemen-
tary School. It was right in the Aarons' neighborhood,
and Blunt can remember Henry hanging around the
field when he was three or four years old. "He used
to carry my glove," says Blunt, who was about eighteen
at the time. "Sometimes we would play with him, let
him throw the ball. Even then, he threw the ball more
like a man than a child."

Henry wished his father would take him to Council
Field on a Saturday or a Sunday, for he knew he would
get more chance to play if he was with his father. But
his father was busy trying to make a living for his family, and he took any chance for weekend work at the
company because of the overtime pay. There were very
few games of catch in the backyard for Herbert Aaron
and his son.

There was an uncle, one of Stella Aaron's brothers,
who might have been a fine baseball player if he'd had
a chance. He would play catch with Henry. Another

of his mother's brothers was also a very skilled player, but every time Henry asked him to play catch he said he was too tired.

Once in a while, on a Sunday, Herbert Aaron would take Henry to Hartwell Field in Prichard, a suburb of Mobile, to see the Mobile Bears of the Southern Association play. At that time no black players were allowed in the major leagues, so blacks who loved baseball formed their own leagues. The teams in the Southern Association played each other in cities across the South. They played only on Sundays, and the players received little pay, but they would have played for nothing, merely for the sheer pleasure of playing. They were probably very much like Henry Aaron when they were young.

The players he remembers best were "Shotgun" Shuba and "Four-Sack" Dusack, and he remembers them more because of their nicknames than because of anything he saw them do. "I remember hearing the name Babe Ruth," he recalls, "but I remembered it because of the sound, not because of anything Babe Ruth did. I didn't know if he'd hit seven hundred or eight hundred home runs; I just knew he was someone people talked about."

Despite the fact that his father was usually not around to play with him, despite the fact that the teenage boys on Council Field thought he was too young to play with them, Henry Aaron became a skilled player.

Herbert Aaron recalls, "I'd ask, 'Where is that boy Henry?' and Stella would say, 'You know where he is —out there on that ball field.' Then I'd say, 'I'm going out there to get him.' And Stella would stop me with, 'No, you just leave that boy alone.'"

When the Aarons moved to Edwards Avenue, Henry began to go to Toulminville Recreation Center, which was only a couple of blocks from his home. By the time he was thirteen or fourteen years old, he was playing with adults. "Why, some of those players were twenty-one, twenty-two years old—maybe older," says Mrs. Aaron. "Some of them had families." It was clear that Henry had talent, although some thought he was too small to be a good player. Like his father, he was short and slim.

By this time, Herbert Aaron had taken a greater interest in baseball and found more time to devote to it, not because of Henry's skill but because of Herbert Jr.'s. Mr. Aaron started a sandlot team known as Aaron's Whippets, buying all their equipment and uniforms.

"Cost me about three hundred dollars, which was a lot of money then," he recalls. "Still is a lot of money. But in those years I thought more of Herbert junior's hitting than I did Henry's hitting."

The team consisted chiefly of adults, twenty to twenty-five years old. Herbert Jr. and Henry were the youngest players on the team. Henry, at fourteen, was the team's shortstop. "He could hit the ball then but he couldn't run too fast," Herbert Aaron recalls.

Herbert Jr. would later go into the Army, and he would never regain his hitting skill. Henry, of course, would get better and better.

When baseball wasn't available, Henry played any kind of ball he could find. At Central High School there was only a softball team, so Henry played on it. There was also a football team, and Henry was on that as well. He played so well, in fact, that Florida A & M offered him a scholarship to play football and baseball.

Today Mrs. Aaron says, a little wistfully, "I never did understand football, but it would have been good for him. Florida A and M over at Tallahassee wanted him, and he could have gone to college. I wanted most of all for Henry to go to college, and then have a career, like be a lawyer."

While he enjoyed football, baseball was really the only game for Henry, and when he was offered a chance to play with the Mobile Bears he wanted so much to accept it.

One day Henry was playing third base with his Central High School softball team. To this day, he still does not know what he did that caused a man who was watching to approach him after the game. Obviously he displayed talent, and obviously he had grown big enough to play well.

"How would you like to play baseball and make some money at it?" asked Ed Scott. Henry knew the man; he lived right down the street from the Aarons. He owned the Mobile Bears.

"I don't know, Mr. Scott," Henry answered. "I'd like to, but I'll have to ask my mama. She wants me to get an education."

Ed Scott laughed. It wouldn't interfere with school, he assured Henry. The Bears only played on Sundays.

"That's even worse," Henry sighed. "Sunday is the Lord's day. Mama would never let me play on Sundays."

Ed Scott asked him to think about it and left.

"When Henry asked me if he could play with the adult team, I said no, no, no," his mother recalls. "Mr. Scott was a nice man, but I didn't want my son playing baseball on Sundays.

"The next Sunday, Mr. Scott came looking for Henry. I didn't know where the boy was, and I told Mr. Scott that Henry wasn't going to play baseball for his team. Mr. Scott hung around for a while and then left. When Henry came home, I asked him where he'd been. He said he'd been out playing.

"The same thing happened two more Sundays. Mr. Scott kept telling me how it would be a break for Henry to play for his team. Henry kept coming back home after Mr. Scott left, looking kind of sad and as if he might be expecting something at the same time. By then I knew he was staying away on purpose when Mr. Scott came. I guess he didn't want to be there when I said no.

"The next Sunday, when Mr. Scott came, Henry stayed around, just far enough away so we could see him but not talk to him. Mr. Scott kept talking to me about how good Henry was, and I kept looking at Henry. Finally, I said Henry could play with Mr. Scott's team."

Henry Aaron tried out for the Mobile Bears and made the team, as shortstop. He didn't care what position he played—he just wanted to play baseball. But he did not mind at all when he got paid. The players shared a percentage of the gate receipts. Sometimes each player received as much as ten dollars. "I had never seen that much money in my whole life, all put together," Hank Aaron recalls.

As a sixteen-year-old Sunday player on a Negro baseball team, Henry Aaron had not exactly cracked the big leagues. But he was playing baseball, and that was enough for him.

By the time George Herman Ruth, Jr., was seventeen, he could no longer be considered an "incorrigible." It was true that his periods of stay at home were unsuccessful. Yet it was understandable that he and his father did not get along. They had been practically strangers all of George's life. Mr. Ruth expected his son to obey him like a father. George resented these attempts at authority from a man he did not respect. Sometimes it seemed to him that his father did not want *him* at all, just a helper in the saloon whom he did not have to pay.

St. Mary's was George's real home. It was there that he felt valued as a person. The people there were his family, and Brother Matthias was his father. Babe Ruth often spoke of Brother Matthias as the person most responsible for his growing up with a chance to make it in the world:

"Brother Matthias never lost patience with me, no matter what I did. I think he missed me whenever I'd leave St. Mary's, but he'd make a little ceremony out of each 'parole.' He'd tell me I was on my way, that I'd make a go of things and become a hard-working and industrious part of the community. . . . But, presently, I'd be back again and though I guess he was disappointed he never let me know he was. . . . When I'd have trouble with my studies, or my tailoring work, he'd help me. . . . He taught me to read and write—and he taught me the difference between right and wrong."

George knew he had a lot against him. He knew the people of Baltimore looked down on the boys at St. Mary's. He knew that people in general looked down on a boy who had enjoyed little home life as a child, whose father ran a saloon, who was poor. Yet, through Brother Matthias, George had come to feel that he was valuable as a person. Through St. Mary's, he had learned a trade—tailoring. When he left the school and went out into the world, he would have a skill and could find a job.

Every boy who loves baseball dreams of playing with the pros, and George Ruth was no exception. But he was realistic. He knew there were many skilled young players trying to get into professional ball. He did not know the first thing about breaking into the minor teams, not to mention the majors. No, he might have dreams, but he had no great expectations. He would leave St. Mary's when he was twenty-one and become a tailor.

By the time Henry Aaron was seventeen, he had gone through his own growing-up crises. For one thing, he had taken a middle name. Not having a middle name had bothered him very little when he was young. But as he grew older he found that all his friends had middle names, so he decided to have one too. He took the middle name Louis—not because of Joe Louis, the black boxer who had defeated white boxer James J. Braddock for the world title in 1937, but because he liked the name.

The bigger crisis for Henry Aaron was realizing what it meant to be black in a white society. Herbert Aaron recalls one of the times when it was hard to be a black father:

"One time, Henry and I were sitting on the back steps. I guess he was about twelve years old. We were just talking. An airplane flew by overhead, and Henry said, all of a sudden, 'I'd like to be a pilot.' I said, 'Forget about it, because there are no black pilots.' He looked at me and said, 'Well, I want to be a ballplayer.' I said, 'Well, forget about that, too, because there are no black ballplayers.' I didn't want to put him down, you understand, but when you're a father and you're black, you've got to teach your kids to be realistic."

Henry had begun to understand that kind of realism

by the time he was twelve, but he had not yet accepted it. He was lucky to be born in a time when he would not have to accept it.

About a year later, in 1947, the Brooklyn Dodgers signed Jackie Robinson, the first black player to break into the major leagues. It is hard to explain what that meant to black Americans, especially to black Americans like thirteen-year-old Henry Aaron. His father continued to caution him against hoping to be a career baseball player even after the Robinson breakthrough: "He's just one man, son. Maybe he'll carry a few others in on his coattails, but it will be a long time before major league baseball is really integrated."

But Henry heard and read about Jackie Robinson and hoped. He would not resign himself to graduating from high school and getting just an ordinary job. Once his interest in Jackie Robinson got him into trouble.

"There was a day when business was slow at the company," Herbert Aaron recalls. "I got off work early, and I was walking home, kind of glad to be off but worrying about the money I wasn't making. I was passing by this poolroom, and I just casually looked in, and who did I see inside but Henry. He was supposed to be in school. I stood there, watching him, until finally he must have felt me watching. He turned around, and I crooked a finger. He came out real fast."

Henry was not one to play hooky very often, but that morning, on his way to school, he had passed the poolroom and noticed on the board that the Brooklyn

Dodgers were playing that afternoon, and that the game would be carried on radio. He had decided to listen to the game rather than go to school. He told his father this. He also told his father that he was going to drop out of school if he got a chance to play baseball.

"I didn't punish him," Herbert Aaron recalls. "I just talked to him. His mother and I had worked hard so our kids could get the education we couldn't have. We both had to quit school to go to work to support our families. We didn't want our kids to have to do that. Henry was not going to drop out of school until he was finished."

Henry listened to his father and was moved. He realized how hard his parents had worked to make sure he received a good education, and he determined to finish high school for their sake. While Henry Aaron did indeed get his high school diploma, he did not get it exactly in the way his parents expected.

On February 6, 1914, George Herman Ruth, Jr., turned nineteen. He was six feet two inches tall and weighed one hundred and sixty pounds.

In the middle of February, 1914, George was throwing a baseball around the still frozen yard of St. Mary's when he stopped to watch a group of men approaching. Three he recognized—Brother Matthias, Brother Paul, head of the school, and Brother Gilbert, athletic director of the wealthy private school up the road, St. Joseph's. The other man was introduced to him as Jack Dunn, boss of the Baltimore Orioles of the International League.

Ruth would later recall, "Dunn had heard about me, he said and, to my complete surprise, asked me if I'd like to sign with the Orioles. To me, it was as if somebody had suddenly popped up and asked me to join the United States Senate."

George could not believe his ears. Stunned, he listened to the men talk about the steps that would have to be taken. He was just nineteen, and legally he was in St. Mary's custody until he was twenty-one. Dunn would have to become his legal guardian and be responsible for him until he reached that age. Dunn agreed.

Then salary was mentioned. Dunn said he would start George out at six hundred dollars a year. This was just too much for George to take. A chance to play baseball and be paid for it too! Six hundred dollars was more money than he had ever even imagined. He had to get away to a quiet place where he could rest and let his head stop spinning!

For days after that, George moved as if sleepwalking. He packed what few possessions he had so soon that he kept having to go back into the bag for things he needed. He said good-by to every boy and every brother a dozen times. He could not concentrate on his studies. As hard as he tried, he could not believe what was happening to him. Only when the barred gate of St. Mary's was bolted behind him on February 27, 1914, and he walked away with Dunn did he really believe.

The train ride to the Orioles' spring training camp in Fayetteville, North Carolina, was his first. He would always remember that ride as both his first and his most uncomfortable.

First, he was scared, more scared than he had ever been in his life before: ". . . wondering if I could make the grade and fearful that I'd fail, and be forced to come back to St. Mary's. And that wasn't because I didn't like St. Mary's. I just couldn't have stood the shame of coming back."

Second, he was physically uncomfortable. One of the older players, a catcher named Ben Egan, told him that the little clothes hammock that reached from one end of his berth to the other had been put there for him to rest his pitching arm.

Ruth would remember: "I held my arm up in this uncomfortable position all night, because I wanted to act like a pro. . . . The train pulled into Fayetteville early the next morning with the first Oriole injury of the nineteen-fourteen season. A rookie named Ruth had a cramped and sore pitching arm, thanks to the 'rest' he had carefully given it."

In 1951, when Henry Aaron was seventeen, the Indianapolis Clowns came to Mobile to play the Bears. The Clowns were a barnstorming team, somewhat like the Harlem Globetrotters in basketball. They traveled all over the country to play the best local black teams.

When they came to Mobile in 1951, Henry was playing shortstop for the Bears, and when the game was over the Clowns' secretary, Bunny Downs, approached Henry, asked when he would graduate, and said he would send Henry a contract the next year to play with the Indianapolis Clowns.

Henry thought the man was just talking. But when, the next spring, he received a contract in the mail, he realized Downs had meant what he said.

The arrival of the contract caused great discussion in the Aaron household. Henry still had three weeks left before graduation, and his parents were set upon his getting his diploma. But the contract called for Henry to report to training camp immediately, and it offered him two hundred dollars a month.

"Two hundred dollars a month to play baseball! You can't imagine how big that looked to me, and to my mama, and to my daddy," Aaron recalls.

"I promised that I would come back and get my diploma if they would let me sign with the Clowns. They had misgivings, but finally they gave in."

One morning in May, 1952, Henry, accompanied by his mother, his older brother, Herbert, Jr., and his older sister, Sarah, boarded a train for Winston-Salem, North Carolina, to join the Indianapolis Clowns.

"That is one day I will never forget," says Mrs. Aaron. "We took a cab to the railroad station, and I cried all the way. He had never been away from me before, except to his Granddaddy's farm outside Camden, and he was still just a little boy to me. It was like we were sending him away and we were never going to see him again.

"I had packed him a little lunch. Henry liked fried chicken and banana pudding, but I thought sandwiches would travel better. Anyway, I wasn't sure they would serve a Negro boy on that train. Herbert had given him two dollars. By the time we put him on the train, we were all crying."

George Ruth's train ride from Baltimore, Maryland, to Fayetteville, North Carolina, in 1914 had been his first. Thirty-eight years later, Henry Aaron experienced *his* first train ride, to the Indianapolis Clowns' spring training camp in Winston-Salem, North Carolina.

"I didn't sleep much that night," Hank Aaron recalls. "I spent some of the time just exploring the train. I went through the dining car and found out that my mother was wrong. They would have served me, but it would have cost me more than the two dollars I had in my pocket. I didn't know that people sat down and ate their dinner off a table while the train was moving.

"The rest of the time I was just plain scared. I kept wondering if I shouldn't get off the train and go right back to Mobile. Every time that train pulled into a station, I'd say to myself, 'I'm getting off at the next stop.'"

But Henry Aaron, like George Ruth thirty-eight years before him, was on a train of no return. This was his chance, and scared as he was, he took it.

2 /
Babe and Hank:
Early Years in Baseball

Nineteen-year-old George Ruth got the nickname "Babe" during the first few days at the Orioles' spring training camp in Fayetteville. It came about through a couple of incidents.

One was the first time manager Jack Dunn led his new player out onto the playing field. Dunn had a reputation for finding very young players and developing them. Among the Baltimore team, it was something of a joke that Dunn was always showing up with some baby-faced kid. When Dunn brought his latest find out on the field and to the pitcher's box George was so green, and so awed, that he practically had to be led by the hand.

"Look at Dunnie and his new babe," one of the older players yelled.

While he was thought of as a green "babe," George didn't get the nickname until a few days later. Everything was so new to him that he walked around in a daze. He could not believe, for example, that team members could eat all they wanted, free. For his first breakfast in Fayetteville, to the astonishment of his teammates, he ate three stacks of wheatcakes and three orders of ham. His first few mornings he got up early just to go down to the railroad station and watch the trains go through. The hotel elevator fascinated him. He rode on it every chance he got and carefully watched what the operator did. At last he could not control himself—he bribed the operator to let him run the elevator. He would later recall what happened:

"My playing life, in fact my life, nearly ended a few minutes later. I left a door open on the third floor and was rubbernecking up and down the corridor while I made the elevator go up another flight. Suddenly a player screamed at me to pull my fool head inside, and I did—just in time to keep it from being crushed.

"Dunnie bawled me out until the stuffings ran out of me, and what he didn't say to me the older players said for him. But finally one of them took pity on me, shook his head and said:

"'You're just a babe in the woods.'

"After that they called me Babe."

"Babe" Ruth soon showed his teammates that while he might be green in many ways, he was certainly not green on the field.

"We had a better system of spring training in nineteen fourteen than we have today," Ruth recalled in 1948. "We took our time getting ready to play. . . . Today a player who hasn't gone in for a lick of exercise through the whole winter and spring arrives at training camp just in time to be tossed into a regulation exhibition game. . . . That system and, of course, night ball, is taking years off the playing lives of thousands of modern ballplayers."

The first game the Orioles played in the spring training of 1914 was an intra-squad game. Dunn picked the teams and named them the Sparrows and the Buzzards. Babe played on the Buzzards, first as shortstop and then as pitcher. It was during this game that Babe hit his first professional home run.

It was not a "clinch-hit"—the game did not depend upon it. The Buzzards were ahead of the Sparrows. What made it talked about in baseball circles was the distance.

Babe did not hit at this ball any differently than he did at any other. He watched the pitch closely as it came up to the plate, twisted his body into a backswing, and, swinging as hard as he could, connected.

The ball sped up and out, clearing the right-field fence. Buzzards and Sparrows alike stopped to watch its progress. It landed in a cornfield far beyond the fence. Babe, too, watched the ball's flight as he rounded the bases. At home plate he leaped into the air in excitement! Teammates and opposition players alike crowded around him, and Coach Dunn beamed with pride.

"They estimated that it had carried about three hundred and fifty feet," Ruth later recalled. "I guess that doesn't sound like much in these days of the stitched 'golf' ball, but they said it was pretty sensational for me because I was, first of all, a pitcher, and next, a raw rookie. And this was long before anybody heard of the lively ball, when a guy like Frank Baker could win the title of 'Home Run Baker' with eight to twelve home runs a season."

After the initial excitement, the other players went back to the game. When the game was over and the Buzzards had won, Babe's teammates were happy, but they paid little attention to him. Babe, full of himself after his incredible feat, was disappointed. It was the first of many lessons he would have to learn in humility. In those days, older players made it tough for rookies. There was rarely a word of encouragement. And there was a good deal of resentment against a rookie who looked good.

Even Jack Dunn was spare with his praise, but Babe respected this man and knew Dunn wanted to help him. Cocky as he was, Babe listened carefully to Jack Dunn, and learned much from him.

Eighteen-year-old Henry Aaron got the nickname "Hank" while he was with the Indianapolis Clowns. "Hank" is a common nickname for Henry, so there are no special incidents that led to its use. But a nickname means acceptance, and Henry Aaron had just as hard a time as Babe Ruth, if not harder, in gaining acceptance as a young ballplayer.

If being a rookie on a team like the Baltimore Orioles was hard, being a rookie on a team like the Indianapolis Clowns was doubly hard. Jackie Robinson might have cracked the major leagues, but for most black players their situation did not change.

Babe Ruth and the other Baltimore Orioles stayed in a nice hotel and were served all the food they could eat. Henry Aaron and the other Indianapolis Clowns had much poorer accommodations.

"Kids today just don't know how good they have it during spring training," says Hank Aaron. "They should go through my first spring training with the Clowns in Winston-Salem, North Carolina. We stayed in an old hotel. There was a poolroom on the first floor, and you could hear the men talking and the balls being shot at all hours. The food was bad, and while they would let you have seconds, they looked so grudging that you almost lost your appetite. And everything in town smelled like tobacco. Of course, it was a tobacco town."

On the road, the Baltimore Orioles stayed in good hotels and ate in fine restaurants. The Indianapolis Clowns did not. In those days many hotels and restaurants would not serve blacks, so the bus that took them from game to game served as their hotel.

But even if the hotels and restaurants had been open to them, they would have had little time to take advantage of them. Their schedule was haphazard, made up week by week with many last-minute changes. The Clowns had to accept every game offer just to make ends meet, and sometimes they had to travel forty-eight hours straight to get from one game town to another.

Sometimes when the Clowns had such long distances to travel between games that they spent two days and nights on the bus, they left it only to buy food and to stretch their legs. Among the Indianapolis Clowns, a roommate was not the player with which one shared a room but the man who sat next to him on the bus.

Rookie Aaron soon earned his first fame with his team, as well as with other Negro teams, through his behavior on that bus. While other players killed time by reading, playing cards, or talking, Henry Aaron slept.

"I was known as the sleepingest ballplayer in history," Hank Aaron recalls. "I could sleep anywhere, any time, under any conditions. I slept in the locker rooms, waiting for the bus, on the bus. On a long bus trip, I would sometimes go to sleep as soon as the bus started to roll and sleep practically through until the end of the trip, whether it was six hours or forty-eight hours. My 'roommate' would wake me up when we stopped to get food, and I'd wake up, and go out and buy something and eat it, but then I'd go back to my seat and go to sleep again."

It got to be a team joke. When Henry opened his eyes, his teammates would cheer, "Hank's awake! Hank's awake!" They would use the endearing nickname on the bus, off the field. But it took some time for Henry Aaron to become "Hank" Aaron on the baseball diamond.

The older players on the Clowns first greeted Aaron as the Baltimore players had greeted Ruth. "Like a disease," Hank Aaron recalls. "A new player coming in meant somebody had to go, and, in those days, there weren't too many other places a black ballplayer could go. It was a question of survival."

The first day Henry worked out with the team in Winston-Salem, it was cold. Warm-up jackets were passed out, but the Clowns' camp was so jammed that Henry didn't get one. Shivering, he waited for his turn in the batting cage. After hitting two balls on the line, however, he was chased out, for there were others waiting for batting practice. When he got out on the field, wearing the pair of spikes he'd had for three or four years and a beat-up glove, one of the older players yelled, "Where you get your equipment, kid, from the Salvation Army?" Not until later in the day was Henry given a warm-up jacket and assured that he could have as much time as he wanted in the batting cage.

One reason Henry was given an "in" to the batting cage was that the Clowns' manager, Sid Pollock, wanted him to get over his distressing habit of batting cross-handed. This was easier said than done. Henry, after all, had been batting cross-handed all his life, and it was hard to change. Even though he knew he had to learn to hit properly in order to go farther in baseball, he resisted.

"I knew how I was supposed to hit," he later recalled, "but in a clinch I'd go back to the way I knew best. If I had two strikes on me and my back was to the Clowns' dugout so they couldn't see where my hands were, I'd sneak my left hand back up top. It felt more comfortable in a pressure situation."

The older players thought Henry's unorthodox way of hitting was as funny as his penchant for sleeping. They joked about it a lot. When, in his first time at bat in a regular league game, he hit a home run, they did not joke. When he followed that home run with a single and two doubles in the same game, they stopped joking about his hitting style almost completely. As the days passed and he never went a day without a hit, they started calling him "Hank" on the ballfield as well as off. He got a slot as the club's regular shortstop. While the older players remained suspicious of him, the fact that he became "Hank" to them says a lot about their acceptance of this rookie.

Babe Ruth also had a good hitting as well as pitching record during his first professional games with the Baltimore Orioles. In his very first International League game, played against Buffalo on April 22, 1914, he allowed only six hits, walking four and striking out four. He also got two of the ten Orioles hits. In succeeding games he pitched and hit just as well. Even before midseason the Orioles were far ahead in the International League.

But hardly anyone in Baltimore cared. That year the Federal League arrived in Baltimore, putting up a field right across from the Orioles' park. The Baltimore Federals also began to win early, and the fans left the Orioles in droves to root for the Federals. "The Baltimore Feds would play to twenty thousand and we'd play to twenty," Ruth would later recall. "I'm not kidding."

Fans are essential to the survival of any team in sports, no matter what the game or the league. Fans buy tickets, and ticket money goes for ball park rental, salaries, and other team expenses. In short, no fans, no club. In midseason, 1914, despite the fact that his team was far ahead in the International League, Jack Dunn was forced to sell off the best players on the Baltimore Orioles team. Babe Ruth, along with veterans Ernie Shore and Ben Egan, was sold to the American League's Boston Red Sox, managed by Bill Carrigan.

While Babe had established some reputation in the International League, he was treated by the Red Sox as just another rookie. Naturally he resented this. He felt that he had already proved himself, and he let his new teammates know it. He would later recall:

"I just wanted to show them I was as good as any of the other pitchers Bill Carrigan had. But the thing the older Boston players most resented about me was that I insisted on taking batting practice. One day I came to the park and found that all my bats had been neatly sawed in two. But, generally, I got along okay."

Babe's first experience with the Red Sox was brief. He only joined the club in midseason, too late to help them, if he could have, catch the Athletics in the American League. Meanwhile, however, Providence, the Red Sox team in the International League, had advanced to top position over the crippled Baltimore Orioles. So Babe was sent to the Providence team.

He helped the team win the pennant. It was while he was at Providence that Babe hit his first home run in regular competition. Altogether, in his first season with Baltimore and Providence, Babe had an excellent record. As a pitcher, he won 22 games and lost nine. As a hitter, he had an odd extra base record—two doubles, ten triples, and one homer.

Often during that first professional season Babe thought about Brothers Matthias, Paul, Albert, and Gilbert and the boys with whom he had played baseball who were still at St. Mary's. He knew they were following his progress closely, and he was proud that he was making good for them. The only fan letter he received during the 1914 season came from Brother Matthias, and Babe treasured it. It read simply, "You're doing fine, George. I'm proud of you."

Ruth returned to the Red Sox for the 1915 season, and he returned as a man, by his, the court's, and St. Mary's reckoning. Not until nineteen years later did they all realize they had been off by one year. In 1934 Ruth applied for a passport, and it was only then, when he had to furnish a birth certificate, that he learned that he had been born in 1895 instead of 1894 as he and everyone else had thought.

In baseball terms he was a man anyway, no matter what his age. That season he was the American League's won-lost leader, winning 18 games and losing 6 for a percentage of .750. He struck out 112 hitters and his earned-run record was 2.44. He had an excellent hitting record, too, for a pitcher. In 42 games, in some of which

As a rookie with the Boston Red Sox, Babe Ruth hit all his balls in the same manner. He watched the pitch closely, twisted his body into a backswing, and, swinging as hard as he could, connected. When he *really* connected, it was a sight to see.

(Culver Pictures)

he appeared only as a pinch hitter, his batting average was .315, with 10 doubles, one triple, and four homers.

Yet, with all that, he saw action in the World Series only once that season, and then as a pinch hitter. The 1915 World Series was played between the Boston Red Sox and the Philadelphia Phillies. As the American League's won-lost leader, Ruth naturally expected to pitch. But Bill Carrigan had other plans. He led off with Ernie Shore and then got winning games from George Foster and Dutch Leonard. "I grabbed Carrigan's lapels before each game and demanded to know when I was to get my chance," Ruth would later recall. But each time, Carrigan went with someone else. The only appearance Babe made in that World Series was in the first game, as a pinch hitter. It was the ninth inning, and the Red Sox were trailing 3 to 1. "Here's your chance, Ruth," said Carrigan, and Babe was ready for it. He advanced to the batter's box, waited for a good pitch, and hit it with everything he had. It lined down toward first base, and Babe watched it as he ran after it, thinking it would go past the Phillies' first baseman, Luderus. But Luderus made a great stop and beat him to the bag. That was the end of Babe Ruth's first and last appearance in the 1915 World Series.

Like Babe Ruth, Hank Aaron soon moved from his

When Babe Ruth joined the Red Sox in 1914, he felt he had already proved himself as a pitcher with the Baltimore Orioles. The older Red Sox players, however, treated him as just another rookie. *(Hall of Fame)*

first professional team to his second. The major league scouts followed his career with the Clowns, and shortly the bids started to come in. On the advice of manager Sid Pollock, Hank chose the National League's Milwaukee Braves.

The Braves assigned Aaron to their farm club at Eau Claire, Wisconsin, in the Class C Northern League. Today a player with Aaron's skills might be moved right up to the major league club. But the Braves were taking no chances. Jackie Robinson had opened up the major leagues to ballplayers, and the Braves wanted black players as much as any other team, but Hank Aaron was young, and the Braves felt he needed experience first. Besides, the Eau Claire club was so desperate for a shortstop that Hank was flown up from Charlotte, North Carolina, where the Clowns happened to be, on the day he was sold.

Hank had never flown before. He was so scared he had to be helped onto the plane. During the flight he was sick to his stomach. By the time he arrived at Eau Claire he was a physical wreck. But the Eau Claire team wasn't kidding when they said they needed a shortstop. Hank got off the plane to learn that he was just in time to dress for a ball game.

He may have been sick as a "civilian," but in uniform on the ballfield Hank Aaron was transformed. He got two hits in that first game, one in the second, and more in succeeding games. After only two weeks he made the league all-star team.

He was an okay shortstop, but he was a dynamite

hitter. By this time he had conquered his habit of cross-handed hitting, but he still had a strange stance. It was so strange, in fact, that it broke all the rules of batting. He hit off his left foot—his front foot. Normally, this means that the batter must shift his weight and thus lose power. But not Hank. Despite the fact that each time he swung he shifted his weight instead of keeping his balance, he kept every bit of his power. More than that, he seemed to be able to hit anything. Opposing pitchers tried everything against him, but even when they threw a fast ball right at him it didn't work. He would simply fall away and cream it. His strike zone seemed to extend, as one of his managers later put it, "from the tip of his cap to the tops of his shoes."

Hank Aaron played 87 games with the Eau Claire team that season; if he had not arrived so late, he would have played many more. As it was, he was the unanimous choice as the Northern League's rookie of the year. He was the league's all-star shortstop two weeks after he arrived in Eau Claire, and at the end of the season he was batting .336, scoring 89 runs, getting 116 hits, and driving in 61 runs. He did not lead the league in anything, but he probably would have led it in everything if he had played the entire season.

Hank took the honor in stride. That was partly because of his nature. He was not one to show great emotion, on the field or off. In Eau Claire he had continued his habit of sleeping anywhere; fellow players and sportswriters alike marveled at his ability to sleep in the locker room, even fifteen minutes before a game. He had also become rather famous for taking his time. While he was fast when necessary, as when running the bases, often, when fielding the ball at shortstop, he waited until the last minute before throwing it to first. When asked why he didn't hustle more, he would answer, "My daddy told me never to hurry unless I had to."

At the end of the 1952 season, despite the fact that he had enjoyed a great 87-game streak at Eau Claire, Hank was not moved up to the Milwaukee team. The Milwaukee Braves were loaded with talent already, and they did not want to move a nineteen-year-old up too fast. They moved Hank to Jacksonville, Florida, to play second base with the Jacksonville Tars of the Class A South Atlantic League, under manager Ben Geraghty. He was one of three non-white players to enter the league that season and break the color line. One of the two others, Felix Mantilla, a Puerto Rican, also came to the Jacksonville team in 1953, which was nice for both Hank and Felix. Together they shared the burdens that beset non-white ballplayers in the South at that time. While their teammates slept in one hotel, Hank and Felix found a room across the tracks. While the other Tars ate in restaurants, Hank and Felix waited on the bus for someone to bring them food.

Being a southern black, Hank expected these Jim Crow situations. While he resented them, he took them in stride. Harder to take, somehow, were the epithets on the baseball field. While his white teammates might be called "dummy" or "dope" by opponents' fans, he was always called "nigger." "Get that nigger out of there!"

someone would yell as Hank approached the plate. "Miss that ball, nigger," he would hear as he ran to catch a fly. Even some of the hometown fans seemed to resent his blackness, to consider his presence on the team as a kind of insult. "Nigger! Nigger!" Hank could have complained about it all. Sportswriters were always looking for good

In 1953, when Hank went to the Jacksonville Tars of the South Atlantic League, he was one of three non-white players to break the league's color bar. That season he was named the "Sally" League's MVP. He still considers Ben Geraghty, shown here with him, his best manager. *(United Press International)*

copy, and they would have played up the story, comparing Hank's problems with those of Jackie Robinson when he first broke into the major leagues.

But Hank knew that speaking out on racial issues would do him more harm than good at that time. He had several ambitions. One was to play in the major leagues. Another was to win the Most Valuable Player award. The third was to win a batting championship. The fourth was to play in the World Series. When he had achieved some or all of these goals, he figured, he would speak out on some of the things that bothered him. At nineteen, though, and as a black, he knew that his speaking out would mean little.

He still had a long way to go before he reached his goals, and this was made clear to him during his 1953 season with the Tars. While he led the South Atlantic League in practically all hitting departments, in runs batted in with 125, in runs scored with 115, in hits with 208, in total bases with 338, and in doubles with 36, he also led in most errors for a second baseman. That's when he became an outfielder. His worst performance, however, occurred as a runner. "It's kind of embarrassing to remember," says Hank Aaron. "I got to first on a hit and stole second, but I walked away from second a little too far. The second baseman threw to the pitcher, and I was tagged out.

"The next time I was up I got a single, and I stole second base again. I slid in, and when I got up I dusted myself off. The trouble was, I stepped off the base to do it. Once more, I was tagged. This time, when I walked back to the dugout, I didn't look at Geraghty.

"The next time at bat, I hit another single, and again I slid into second base. I jumped up, and without asking for time out, I moved off again. I was picked off for the third time.

"It happened again in the eighth inning. I wanted to hide somewhere. I would have gone anywhere except back to the dugout.

"Geraghty was waiting for me. 'Once I can forgive,' he said. 'Twice is bad. Three times is carelessness. Four times is *ridiculous!*'"

The nice thing about Geraghty, though, was that he would not have bawled Hank out that way if the team had lost. He knew Hank felt bad, but he didn't add insult to injury. The Tars won that game. If they had lost, he knew Hank would have been bawling himself out more than his coach could ever do. That is why, to this day, Hank remembers Ben Geraghty as the best coach he ever had.

Needless to say, Hank Aaron would never again be caught off base by a fielder holding the ball after he had stolen.

Babe Ruth saw more and more action each succeeding season with Boston. In 1916 he won 23 games and lost 12, which was an excellent record for a young pitcher. He wanted very much to pitch in the World Series against the Brooklyn Dodgers and this time Bill Carrigan consented. The series opened in Boston on Saturday, October 7. Boston pitcher Ernie Shore worked that first game, which the Red Sox won. There was no Sunday ball in Boston in those days, and Babe got his first chance to pitch a Series game on Monday, October 9. It made the record books as the longest World Series game in history—14 innings! It was so dark by the last inning that the players could hardly see the ball. Babe won that game 2 to 1, and he provided some valuable hitting strength as well, driving in a tying run in the third inning to make the score 1–1. It took eleven long innings after that before the Red Sox scored a run to break the tie.

Babe was exhausted but ecstatic. He had pitched in a World Series game and he had won! Amid the whoops and hollers in the Red Sox clubhouse, he yelled to Carrigan, "I told you a year ago I could take care of those National League bums for you, but you never gave me a chance."

If the Series had gone six games, Babe would have pitched a second time, but Boston shut out the Brooklyn Dodgers in five games, winning the Series 4 to 1.

By the time the 1917 season opened, the Red Sox had gone through some unsettling changes. Bill Carrigan, the manager whom Babe would always put at the top of his list, retired. As if that were not bad enough, the owner of the Boston club, Joe Lannin, sold the Red Sox to Harry Frazee, a New York theatrical man. Then, right at the beginning of the season, the Red Sox almost lost Babe Ruth.

It was June 23 and Babe was pitching against the

Washington Senators. Washington's lead-off man, Eddie Foster, was at bat, and the umpire, Brick Owens, called four straight balls.

"I growled at some of the early balls," Ruth would later recall, "but when he called the fourth one on me I just went crazy."

Babe rushed over to Owens and told him he should go to bed at night so he could keep his eyes open in the daytime. Owens retorted that if Babe didn't shut up he'd be thrown out of the game.

"Throw me out of this game and I'll punch you right in the jaw!" Babe yelled.

Owens threw Babe out of the game, and Babe hauled off and belted him, hard.

"Ban Johnson, then the American League's president, was very easy on me," Ruth stated many years later, in 1948. "I was fined only one hundred dollars and suspended for ten days. They'd put you in jail today for hitting an umpire."

After his suspension, Babe returned to the team and had his second 23-game winning season. While the Red Sox lost out to the Chicago White Sox for the American League pennant, Babe Ruth was becoming well known as a double 23-game winning pitcher who could hit too. He decided to capitalize on his fame by investing in a small Boston cigar factory. It put out a Babe Ruth cigar, which sold fantastically well.

But Babe, too, had his share of troubles with opposing teams' fans. Sports fans are perhaps the cruelest group of all when it comes to picking the names and epithets that can hurt a person most. Babe, with his round, flat-nosed, tanned face, was almost immediately tagged "ape," "baboon," and worse. More often than not, he was called "nigger." Nigger this, nigger that. The insults against Babe along this line were, at times, practically as bad as Jackie Robinson would endure years later and, still more years later, as players like Hank Aaron would face. It got to the point where people started thinking perhaps Babe was part black and that one of his ancestors had "passed" over to white society. The rumor became as strong as the rumor that he was an orphan, and of course the orphan rumor only strengthened the black ancestry rumor.

Babe himself treated everyone, rich and poor, black and white, with the same rough, open friendliness.

The years 1914–1918 saw additional upheavals for the Red Sox as well as for professional baseball in general. The United States entered World War I and many players either enlisted or were drafted into the armed services. Babe had gotten married during his first year as a Red Sox regular and was thus deferred. He joined a National Guard unit and kept on playing. But there was so much shifting and moving of players that in the 1918 season Babe found himself a part-time outfielder. Manager Ed Barrow decided he needed Babe's hitting strength more than his pitching, and while a pitcher only got to play about one out of every four games, an outfielder could play every game.

Babe played 95 games that 1918 season, getting 95 hits, 26 doubles, 11 triples and 11 home runs, for a .300

average. "Today the bat boy hits eleven home runs," Ruth said in 1948, "but in nineteen-eighteen it was good enough to get me a tie with 'Tillie' Walker of the Athletics as the leading home-run hitter of the American League."

The Red Sox were in the World Series again that year, against the Chicago Cubs, and Barrow decided on a clever strategy. In the opening game he surprised the Cubs, and nearly everyone else, by putting Babe in as a pitcher. Chicago, and most everyone else in the league, had thought Babe had given up pitching for hitting. Babe won that first game as well as the other 1918 Series game that he pitched. The Red Sox won the series, four games to two. Babe helped win the fourth game with his very first World Series hit, which drove in two runs.

It happened in the fourth inning. The Red Sox had two men on base, and Babe was up. He was itching to get a hit, for he had not made a World Series hit up to this time in ten times at bat. Manager Ed Barrow gave him his head. "Play your own game, Babe. I don't know whether they'll let you hit or not." Babe went out to face the Cubs' pitcher, George Tyler.

"I thought Tyler intended to pass me when he served up three straight balls, all quite wide of the plate," Ruth would later relate. "Then he slipped me a slow curve. It wasn't good baseball for me to hit at a three and nothing pitch, but Barrow had told me to win my own game and I took a cut at it. I missed it about a foot and the crowd groaned. I let the next one go by, but Brick Owens, the umpire I had slugged in nineteen-seventeen, called it strike two. Tyler looked me over for a long time, then tried to sneak over a fast ball for a third strike. But I was doing some looking myself. The ball came over waist high. I swung from my heels and rammed it over Flack's head in right field, for a triple, scoring Whiteman and Innis."

Babe never reached home, but he was well satisfied with a triple for his first World Series hit.

The Red Sox talked about that clinch triple for many years after, but they talked and laughed longer at an incident that had become typical of Babe Ruth. He was never very good at remembering names. While he was with Baltimore he roomed with a guy named Pippin, but he could not remember the man's name as long as they roomed together. Nearly everyone, to Babe, was Kid. In the clubhouse before the first game in the 1918 series, which Babe pitched, Ed Barrow called special attention to Les Mann, one of the Cubs' outfielders. Mann was a real threat to left-handed pitchers, and Barrow cautioned Babe to be very careful of him. In fact, Barrow advised, it wouldn't hurt to throw one in close to "dust him off a bit" in order to back him off the plate.

The first Chicago hitter Babe faced was a left-hander who stood right up on the plate. Remembering Barrow's advice, Babe threw the ball at him, to back him off. The ball hit the batter in the middle of the forehead!

"I guess I took care of that Mann guy for you," Babe said to Barrow at the end of the inning, and was astonished to see his manager laugh so hard he almost fell off the bench.

"Babe, you wouldn't know General Grant if he walked up there with a bat," cried Barrow.

Babe had hit Max Flack, not Les Mann!

When Hank Aaron reported for spring training in 1954, the Braves' manager, Charles Grimm, wished there were a place for him on the team. But the Braves' lineup was set, and as the team had finished second in the league the year before, they weren't about to change anything. Once training was over, there was nothing to do but send Hank to Toledo, Ohio, to play yet another season in the minors.

As for Hank, he did not seem to worry about the situation, or at least he didn't show it. As always, he slept what seemed incredible hours to those around him. Some claimed he even dozed at the plate and out on the field. Yet they knew he couldn't really be dozing. Out on the field, even though he never seemed to run hard enough to get a ball, he was always under it when it came down. Even though he seemed to wait too long to throw the ball infield, he almost always got the runner. At the plate, too, he proved he was awake. His first time at bat, in a spring exhibition game, he hit a double off Carl Erskine of the Dodgers, a good pitcher. Later in the spring he hit a homer off Curt Simmons of the Phillies, a better pitcher. Grimm watched twenty-year-old Hank and groaned. He hated to send the kid to Toledo, but there was no way around it.

Then, on March thirteenth, a way developed. Bobby Thomson, the Braves' left fielder, broke his leg in three

Hank's hitting sometimes overshadowed his talent in the field. Among those who really knew baseball, however, he developed a reputation as one of the best all-around ballplayers in the game.
(United Press International)

places sliding into second base during an exhibition game against the Yankees. One look at the leg and Grimm knew Thomson was out for the season. The rest of the Braves thought Grimm would put Aaron right in at Thomson's position. Instead, Grimm moved Andy Pafko, the right fielder, over to left field, and announced that Hank and another player, James Pendleton, were up for the right field job. Hank won the contest hands down.

"The next day," Aaron recalls, "I got two hits against the Phillies. And the day after that I hit a triple against the Yankees. The ball went to dead center field over the head of their center fielder, Irv Noren. The next time I got up, Noren decided he'd be smart. He moved 'way out, about four hundred and fifteen feet. I saw him moving out there, so I hit a single to center so far in front of him that I almost made two bases on it."

Hank Aaron is much more talkative now than he was then. In fact, he was so un-talkative that he was a real puzzle to sportswriters. He answered their questions with as few words as possible and in a manner that puzzled them even more. They could never tell whether he was joking or not.

After he had played a few days in the outfield, Hank was asked how he liked it. "I like it fine," he said. "There's less to do—especially thinking." The reporter looked at him sharply, but Hank looked innocently back at him; his expression had not changed a bit.

Hank was scared to death on opening day of the Braves' 1954 season, at Cincinnati, and his hitting showed

When the Milwaukee Braves left fielder, Bobby Thomson, broke his leg in the spring of 1954, Hank and another rookie were in line for the spot. Five days later, on March 18, Hank hit a homer off the Philadelphia Phillies. Manager Charley Grimm shook his hand as he rounded third. Hank won the spot on the team.

(United Press International)

it. He struck out twice, grounded out, hit into a double play, and fouled out. The Reds won, 9–8. Both Hank and the rest of the Braves picked up steam as the season continued. By April 23 they were third in the league.

On that day, Milwaukee went to St. Louis for a series with the Cardinals. Vic Raschi was pitching for St. Louis, and it was off him that Hank got his first major league home run.

"That was a wild game," Aaron remembers. "It went fourteen innings. The score was four-four at the end of the ninth. I hit a single to drive in our fifth run in the thirteenth, but the Cards tied it up in the top of the inning. In the fourteenth, I was up with one man on base. Raschi pumped one of his fast balls in to me, and I hit it with all I had. It went into the left field seats. Man, that was one of the happiest days of my life."

The Braves won that game, 7–5. In seven times up, Hank had two singles and a home run, his best day until then. Two days later he did even better. In six times up, he had a home run and four singles, pacing the Braves to a 12–3 win over the Cardinals in the last game of the series.

Hank also made some memorable mistakes in his rookie season, a couple of which could stand, in baseball annals, with the hilarious acts of the Brooklyn Dodgers of the 1920s, who once had three men on third!

He hit what would have been a double in one game, and, running with his head down, decided to try for a triple. The trouble was, he did not see that the man running from third had decided not to try to score. Instead he turned and made back for the base. The third baseman found himself with a man sliding into base from both directions. He tagged them both out.

Another time, Hank was on first when the batter hit a line drive to right field. Hank was off and running, rounded second, and was making for third when his cap flew off his head. He stopped short and retrieved his cap, then realized that the infield was after him. He could have scored easily, but he was lucky to reach third safely.

Despite such mistakes, Hank matured greatly during that first major league season. By early September the Braves were in third place, but they were only five games behind the first-place Giants. They lost the first game of a double-header against Cincinnati and were ahead 9–7 in the second when Hank came up for his fifth time at bat. He hit a pitch into deep left center and knew it could be a triple. He rounded first, touched second, and barreled toward third. The ball was on its way to Chuck Harmon, the Reds' third baseman, and Hank slid in, completing the triple.

But he slid too hard, breaking his ankle. The rookie who had gotten a spot on the team because the regular left-fielder had broken his leg was carried off the field and out of the season on a stretcher. That was the end of the Braves' pennant hopes.

Hank batted .280 and hit 13 home runs that season and was the Milwaukee baseball writers' unanimous choice for Braves' Most Valuable Player. He did not win any national honors. He ran a poor second to Wally Moon of the Cardinals for the National League's rookie of the year. In 1954 no one was comparing him as a hitter to Babe Ruth. Yet in thinking about Hank Aaron, sportswriters sometimes recalled Babe Ruth's inability to recognize names and faces.

It was not that Hank could not remember names or faces of the pitchers he came up against; he simply did not think they were important. Or so it appeared. Then again, maybe he was just putting the reporters on. In his early years in the majors, Hank was uncomfortable with reporters, and he shielded himself with his dry humor. Nevertheless, legends grew up about his unawareness of people around him.

During his rookie spring training with Milwaukee, Hank hit a homer off Robin Roberts the first time he faced the Phillies pitcher. After the game he was asked by reporters, "What did you think of Roberts?"

"Who?" said Hank.

"Roberts," one of the reporters said, more loudly in case Hank hadn't heard the first time.

"Was that Roberts?" Hank is supposed to have asked.

Anecdotes like this are part of the Hank Aaron legend.

3 /
Babe and Hank:
Superstars

Babe Ruth made baseball history on April 4, 1919. On that day the Red Sox met the Giants in an exhibition game in Tampa, Florida. Twenty-four-year-old Babe, in his first time at bat, hit the longest home run he, or anyone else, had ever hit.

"I don't remember what he [Giants' pitcher George Smith] threw me but it looked awful fat coming up there," Babe would later recall. "There was a little rail fence out in deepest right field. The ball I hit never rose more than thirty feet off the ground, and Ross Youngs, the classic Giant outfielder, rode out with it until he looked like a little boy running after a bird. The ball cleared the fence and then kept rolling."

Observers and players alike paced off the distance the ball had traveled. They brought out a tape measure and measured the distance. They could not believe the result —579 feet! This guy had power! How many homers could he hit if Barrow played him every day?

Babe gave them a taste of the answer early in the 1919 season. He had been asked by Barrow if he wanted to pitch or play outfield. Babe answered that he liked to hit, and he played most of the games in the outfield. In one of the first games he hit a homer with the bases full, the first time he had ever hit a grandslam homer.

After that Babe went into a terrible slump. A month into the season he was batting only .180. There had been no other homers since the one grand slam. But then, just as suddenly as he had gone into the slump, he got out of it. His average soared from .180 to .325 in less than a month, and he was hitting home runs again.

The American League record at the time was 16 homers, made by "Socks" Seybold of the Kansas City Athletics in 1902. The recognized major league record was 25, held by Buck Freeman of the 1899 Washington National League club. Home runs were regarded as a nice "plus," but no one had ever gotten enough of them to focus much attention on "the homer." Then Babe Ruth came along, and as he hit one home run after another, "the homer" suddenly started to get attention, and so did the Babe.

A love song titled "Along Came Ruth" was popular at the time, and sportswriters started to use the phrase to describe times when Babe came through in a clinch. They used it when they wrote about the game against the Yankees when Ruth hit his second grand slam of the year. They used it again when Babe hit two homers in one game for the first time.

By the middle of July, Babe had 11 home runs, equaling his 1918 total. On July 18 he again hit two homers in one game. The second was hit in true "along came

Ruth" fashion. Cleveland was ahead 7–4, and Babe came up in the ninth inning with the bases loaded. His grand slam gave the Red Sox an 8–7 victory. July was great for Babe, who hit nine home runs during the month. The last, on July 29, was his sixteenth, and it tied Seybold's 1902 record.

He just kept on hitting those homers. By August 17 his total was 19, and there seemed no stopping him. But a few days later Babe was, indeed, nearly stopped. The Red Sox were in Cleveland. The umpire was none other than Brick Owens. Owens made a strike call that Babe didn't like and Babe cursed at him. Owens threw him out of the game, and Babe started for him. For a moment the fans and the other players thought they were going to see a replay of the Ruth-Owens debacle of 1915. But Babe's teammates grabbed him and pulled him away.

Except for having to sit out that game, Babe was not penalized in any way. The next day in Detroit he hit his twentieth home run and his fourth grand slam of the season, setting a record that was not broken for forty years. As Babe passed Freeman's home run mark, someone with a lot of patience went through all the old box scores and came up with another record—27 home runs hit by Ed Williamson of the Chicago White Stockings in 1884. Babe took it all in stride. On September 20 he tied Williamson's record. By then he was being called The Mauler.

Babe finished the 140-game season (shorter than usual because of the ending of the war) with 29 home runs, an unheard-of total for the time, and a new star had been born. Fans all over the country waited eagerly for the arrival of morning newspapers to read of Ruth's prowess. Sportswriters filled column after column with anecdotes about him. He was a national sensation.

Despite Babe's home-run hitting, 1919 was not a good season for Boston, which finished in sixth place. There were a lot of problems behind the scenes. The Red Sox, cocky from their two previous pennant wins, were careless. Pitcher Carl Mays quit, complaining that the others were not backing him up on the field. Frazee, pressed for money, sold Mays and two other players to the Yankees.

While he was disappointed with his club's record, Babe Ruth was overjoyed with his own. The poor kid from Baltimore basked in his fame. He went on a postseason tour across the country, appearing in exhibition games, endorsing commercial products, being wined and dined. He was twenty-four years old, and he was sitting on top of the world.

Hank Aaron certainly did not make history during the baseball season of 1956, but he made the baseball world very much aware of him. Actually, interest in him had begun during the season of 1955. By midseason he was batting .340, and while he ended the season with a .314 average, pitchers on opposing teams had come to consider him a serious threat. In fact, pitchers in the league came up with a new nickname for him—Bad Henry. They just did not know how to handle him, and that made him even more dangerous than a batter who might have a higher average but who was more predictable. Their fears were confirmed in the 1956 season.

Hank started out with a tremendous spring training, much the same as Ruth had in 1919. Then, like Ruth, he went into a slump, dropping from over .400 'way down to .167. While he was chosen to play in his second All-Star game (the first was in 1955, and he was one of the stars), he played only a couple of innings and got to the plate only once.

Right after the All-Star game he started hitting again, slowly at first, then picking up steam. It started with one single in three times at bat in a game against the Pittsburgh Pirates on July 15. The next day he got two hits, one a homer. The next day he went two-for-five, including a three-run homer. In the third week of July, in a four-game series against the Philadelphia Phillies, Hank had two singles and a homer in game number one, a single and a double in game number two, a double and a game-winning homer in number three, and a single in the last. His average was then .336, and he was truly "Bad Henry!"

By August 8 Hank's hitting streak was being talked about everywhere in the baseball world. The twenty-two-year-old had hit safely in 25 straight games, and while that was far away from Joe DiMaggio's 56-game record, it was well in sight of the 37-game National League record set by Tommy Holmes of the 1945 Boston Braves. Would Aaron break the National League record?

Not that year. Hank's streak was halted at 25. He took it in stride. Of course he cared, but he had not allowed himself to feel pressured. He had not gotten all excited about the streak, and so he wasn't all upset about its end. "A streak is just luck. And you can't control luck," he said. "Why waste time worrying about something you can't control?"

While Hank's streak may have been halted, his good hitting continued, and he was a clear contender for the league batting championship. Meanwhile the rest of the Braves had also been hitting well, and by the middle of August they knew they had a shot at the National League championship. At that point the Braves were in a three-way tie for first place with the Cincinnati Reds and the Brooklyn Dodgers. Even though the season was still young, the three teams began to play as if they were in the home stretch. The pressure was especially evident when one of the three teams played another. At least it was evident in all the players except Hank Aaron.

One day the Braves were playing the Reds and Hank was at bat. A pitch from Cincinnati was called a ball by the home-plate umpire, and Cincinnati catcher Smokey Burgess did not agree. The two got into a heated argument. Hank stood there and listened for a few moments, then turned to Burgess and said, "Kindly do not agitate the arbiter. He can't be as pluperfect as you are."

Umpire and catcher looked at Hank in astonishment, then broke into gales of laughter. Play was resumed.

By the middle of September, the Reds had dropped back and the Dodgers had moved up to within half a game behind the Braves. Then, on the next to last day of the season, the Dodgers won a double-header against the Pittsburgh Pirates and the Braves lost to the Cardinals. Only a Braves win and a Dodgers loss could save the Braves, and while they won their last game against the Cardinals, the Dodgers also beat the Pirates in their last game. That was the end of the Braves' pennant hopes.

The team was terribly disappointed, and none of them was more disappointed than Henry Aaron. He had enjoyed a good season, winning the league batting championship with a .328 average and distinction both as the only man in the league to have 200 hits and as the league leader in doubles. He became, at twenty-two, the second youngest batting champion in National League history, and he was not second youngest by much. Pete Reiser of the 1941 Dodgers was only a month and a half younger when he won the title.

But all these were somehow hollow victories for Hank. He would rather have had his team win the pennant.

Babe Ruth was sold to the New York Yankees early in January 1920. Boston owner Frazee hated to do it, of course, but former Red Sox owner Joe Lannin was demanding payment on notes that Frazee had given him when he had bought the Red Sox. For his part, Babe

(Top) Probably the most famous home run Babe Ruth ever hit was in the World Series of 1932. Lou Gehrig, number 4, is next at bat as Ruth scores. (Bottom) Here the Babe autographs a rubber ball for a young fan in the Rainbow Hospital in Cleveland in 1934.   *(Private collection)*

hated to go. He had become settled in Boston and liked the town and the people he knew there. But he loved baseball, and he would have played hard for any team. Later, of course, he came to regard New York as his home and himself as, first and foremost, a Yankee.

Much excitement accompanied the opening of the Yankees' spring exhibition games that year, and much speculation preceded the regular season. Was the Babe's fantastic 29-home-run record just a fluke, or could he really do it again? Fans jammed the bleachers at exhibition games in the South and filled the Polo Grounds in New York to find out.

At first Babe disappointed them. During a spring training series with the Brooklyn Dodgers he struck out two or three times a game. The record number of New York reporters covering the Yankees' camp in Jacksonville, Florida, wrote pieces with headlines like "Babe Strikes Out with the Bases Filled," and "Babe Fizzles in the Pinch." Babe got angry, and shortly he began to hit again.

By midseason Babe had matched the 29-home-run record of 1919, and from then on each additional homer meant a new record. And there was no one around to break Babe's record but Babe himself. Altogether, he broke his own record 25 times that season, ending up with the unheard-of season total of 54 home runs!

He finished the season with a .376 average and, in addition to his homers, with 36 doubles, 9 triples, 156 runs, and 137 runs driven in.

While the Yankees did not win the pennant that year, the New York sportswriters had plenty of copy. There were no more headlines like those in the spring. Now the headlines were, "Ruth Hits 40" and "Ruth Saves Game."

While the Yankees were disappointed that they did not get the pennant, they and their backers were very happy about that season's gate receipts. They were the highest in baseball history. "There's something about a home run," Ruth said twenty-eight years later. "Our long knocks, and the race we made of it up to the last minute, enabled the Yanks that year to draw the un-heard-of attendance of 1,289,422 at the Polo Grounds, which then had a capacity of only 33,000. We also were a wonderful draw on the road. No matter where we went the fans swarmed out to see 'Baby Ruth,' as some called me, hit home runs."

Home-run fever, as it came to be called, would radically change baseball.

When the 1957 season opened, all eyes in the world of baseball were on Hank Aaron and the Milwaukee Braves. The Braves, who had barely lost out in the pennant race the year before, seemed a sure winner that year. They had everything—pitching, power, defense, speed; and they had Hank Aaron.

Certainly no one was comparing Hank Aaron with Babe Ruth in 1957, but they were comparing him with hitters like Stan Musial and Willie Mays and Rogers Hornsby. With all that, many were surprised when Braves manager, Fred Haney, put Hank in the number two batting spot.

Hank, as was his fashion, did not complain publicly about the position. "I'm no cleanup batter," he said to reporters who asked him how he felt about Haney's decision. "I'll never drive in one hundred home runs batting second, but there are a few others guys on the team who can do that, and the team is what's important."

Yet, a reporter who knew Hank could sense his disappointment, especially when he said things like, "I just want to play good baseball this season, but I wouldn't mind driving in a hundred runs."

Fortunately, Haney changed his mind two weeks into the season and put Hank in the cleanup spot, where he should have been from the beginning. By the time the Braves had played 59 games, Aaron had hit 19 home runs, and the season was still young. "Maybe I'll hit thirty-five," Hank told reporters.

By July he was approaching 30. "Maybe I'll hit forty," he said.

Meanwhile the Braves were playing excellent ball— until the All-Star game. After the All-Stars, in which Hank played for the third consecutive year, the Braves went into a slump. They picked up just in time to see Hank Aaron sprain his ankle in an important game against Philadelphia.

The doctor said he would be out for two weeks. Hank was ready for play in eight days. The Brooklyn Dodgers arrived in Milwaukee for a three-game series. Henry hit a two-run homer in the ninth to win the first game. The next day, in the first game of a double-header, he hit a three-run homer and then a two-run double to win the game. In the second game of the double-header, he doubled in the eighth inning to tie the score, then scored the winning run on a teammate's single.

By Labor Day the Braves were six and a half games ahead of the second-place team. By September 15 they had dropped eight of their last eleven games. The slump was so bad, sportswriters were predicting that Milwaukee had lost their pennant chance. Then, along came Henry.

Led by his bat, the Braves fought back and, late in September in a game against the St. Louis Cardinals, clinched the pennant with Henry's 44th home run of the season. Sportswriters noted that in 1952 Hank had played with the number 5, had not liked it, had chosen the number 44, and had worn that number ever since. Now, they said, they knew why.

The Braves faced the Yankees in the World Series that year, and this time they won. Hank was happy. He wanted nothing more than that his team win.

In midwinter of that year, Hank received an additional glory. The Baseball Writers of America voted him the National League's Most Valuable Player over Stan Musial.

For Henry, that was an additional and crowning glory. Not only had his team won, but also he had won.

"I think this is the greatest thrill of all for me," he said. "To be on a winning team puts you on top of the world, but being the MVP sort of puts a guy on the baseball honor roll permanently."

Little did he know that one day he would claim a much higher place on baseball's honor roll.

Babe Ruth hit 59 home runs for the Yankees in the

1921 season, passing Roger Connor's lifetime homer record of 136 with his total of 163. That year, the Yankees won the American League pennant, the first in the team's eighteen-year history. Although they later lost the World Series to the National League's New York Giants, the Yankees probably got more publicity than the Giants. Or, rather, one Yankee did. Fifty-nine home runs—the baseball world was aghast. "They thought my fifty-four of nineteen-twenty was such an unheard-of accomplishment that no one again could ever push it up that high," Ruth later recalled.

The fact that someone, even Babe Ruth, could and did caused a lot more Americans to start going out to the baseball parks and caused a lot of baseball team owners and managers to start eyeing the home run as the greatest money-maker in history.

In 1921 *Literary Digest* magazine called the home run an epidemic. It went on to say, "The home-run epidemic might better be called the Babe Ruth epidemic, for the habit began with the so-called and very much admired 'Bambino.'"

Quoting a baseball critic of the day, it continued, "He has batted home runs at so dizzy a pace that he has fired the enthusiasm of the entire country. He has not only slugged his way to fame but he has got everybody else doing it. The home-run fever is in the air."

Baseball club owners capitalized on this home-run fever. Babe Ruth was drawing amazing crowds to Yankee games. If other players could hit home runs, they, too, would draw large crowds to games. During the next few years, through the owners' influence, baseball equipment manufacturers began to make livelier balls—smaller, harder, stitched like those we know today—and bats with all the wood up in the big end and very slender handles. Also through the owners' influence, new rules were introduced to govern the kinds of pitches a batter would face. Trick pitching deliveries like the spitball, the emery ball, the shine ball, and the mud ball were outlawed.

For their part, the Yankee owners did what they could to capitalize on their star's fame. In 1923 the Yankees moved from the old Polo Grounds to the brand-new Yankee Stadium. It was expressly designed as a showcase for the Babe's talents, and, in fact, it became known as "the house that Ruth built." While a pop fly could reach the Polo Grounds seats if it was just inside the foul line, the fences slanted away abruptly to a depth of 475 feet. In the stadium, the entire right-field section 'way out beyond the bull pen was in range for a left-handed pull hitter. By the time Yankee Stadium was opened, however, the whole baseball world had come down with home-run fever.

Other batters began to hit homers. In 1918 the major league home-run total had been only 235; in 1922 there were 1,055. By the end of 1924, Babe's 1919 total of 29 homers seemed fairly modest, for 30 or more home runs in a season had been hit nine times.

But Babe Ruth was still Home Run King. While in 1922 he lost out to Ken Williams' 39 homers, getting only 35, he probably would have led that year as well. He was suspended from the Yankees because he had broken

Three of baseball's all-time greats in 1927. On the left, Ty Cobb, the king throughout his twenty-four-year career. In the center, Babe Ruth, King of Swat. On the right, Eddie Collins, whose brilliant twenty-five-year career is still the longest on record.

(Culver Pictures)

A Yankee outfield combination that sent many pitchers to the showers—Babe Ruth and Bob Meusel.   *(Culver Pictures)*

a rule forbidding players on championship clubs to play promotional games after the World Series, and thus he lost the first 39 days of the season. And while 30 or more home runs in a season had been hit nine times by the end of the 1924 season, Babe's hitting accounted for five of those times.

The meaning of all this was not lost on Babe. He began to live in a manner befitting a "Home Run King."

He would later recall, "I decided I should not stay at the same hotels as the rest of the club, because I usually had a lot of fair-weather friends (who seemed good, at the time) on my neck. In Washington, for instance, the Yanks stayed in three-dollar rooms at the Willard. But not Babe, the Boy Spender. I stopped at the Raleigh, in a hundred-dollar-a-day suite. And travel with the Yanks on short hops? Nothing doing! . . . with the Yanks, I had a long, low Packard roadster, painted a fire-engine red, and there wasn't any greater thrill in life for me than stepping on that baby's gas."

Despite all this, Babe Ruth could never be called a snob. Babe liked everybody and everybody liked Babe, sometimes in spite of themselves.

By 1958 Henry Aaron was a star in his own right, although perhaps the most low-keyed star in baseball history. Those who knew baseball followed his career with great interest. Those who just liked baseball became interested in him as he approached important season batting marks or league records. In between they kind of forgot about him, only to follow his games with renewed interest when the air of excitement in the baseball world signaled the approach of something big.

Hank had a shaky start in 1958, but he finished the season better than his team did. The Braves—cocky, some said, from their 1957 World Series win—lost out to the New York Yankees for the World Championship. Hank finished the season with 30 home runs, his second-best total, 95 RBI's, his third-best total, and an average of .326, which put him fourth in the National League.

In 1959 he got off to a fantastic start, and the baseball world was again abuzz. If he could be hitting over .500 after the first three weeks of the season, maybe he could finish out the season with a .400 average. The last to do that had been Ted Williams in 1941. Babe Ruth had never hit .400. Could Hank Aaron do it?

Hank did everything he could to maintain an over .400 average. He even stopped going to movies, to save his eyesight. But he refused to speculate about it.

Reporters would ask, "Hank, do you really think you can hit four hundred?"

"I don't know," Hank would answer. "I guess we'll just have to wait and see. Right now, I'm aiming for a thousand hits. I've got nine hundred and ninety-eight already. I'd rather aim for a practical goal like that."

Hank did indeed collect his thousandth hit, off the Dodgers, and at age twenty-five became the second youngest ballplayer in big league history to reach that total. Only Ty Cobb of the Tigers was younger, getting one thousand hits when he was twenty-four.

Hank's hitting dropped off in August, and while he

got hot again at the end of the season, the .400 average was beyond his reach. He kept a .355 average to win the National League batting title, however, and he also led the league in hits, total bases, and hitting percentage.

In 1960 Hank had what he considered a bad year, hitting for only a .292 average. Yet he hit more home runs—40—than he had in any previous season, and led the league in RBI's with 126. Many observers wondered how he could consider the season so bad.

Nineteen-sixty was not a very good year for the Braves either. They finished second in the league—again—and attendance at their games was 'way down. It was the third straight year that attendance had dropped since the peak of 1957. Attendance means a great deal for the morale of a ball club, as well as for its profits. When the Braves had arrived in Milwaukee in 1953, the town had welcomed them joyously and rooted for them madly, and with this support the team had worked up to its World Series win in 1957. Now, however, the team was older. The Milwaukee fans took the Braves for granted. Even winning was taken for granted, but at least the fans paid some attention when the team won. When it lost, it was ignored. Even the presence of Hank Aaron did not retain their interest in the team. Certainly he was no showman like Babe Ruth, and at twenty-six he was no longer a rookie to be watched, but his hitting should have counted for something. Sadly, it did not seem to count for enough.

In 1962 Hank got back up into the .300's in batting. While he failed to lead the league in any important category except in doubles, of which he had 39, he did get 34 home runs. He now had a career total of 253 and a lifetime batting average of .319. The only man ahead of him in batting among players with 1000 or more games was Stan Musial.

If the Milwaukee fans did not cheer the Braves' accomplishments as loudly as they could have, Hank's teammates cheered his. Everyone liked Hank and everyone respected his hitting prowess. "He's the greatest hitter in the game," they said over and over. "If it weren't for night baseball, he would hit four hundred every year."

"I changed from batting champion in nineteen twenty-four to the big bust of nineteen twenty-five," Babe Ruth once said. "My batting average caved to two ninety. . . . I hit only twenty-five homers and Bob Meusel (also a Yankee) dethroned me as home-run king." The Yankees, as a team, nose-dived to seventh place, the only time the club had finished in the second division in thirty years.

No team is a one-man team, and Babe cannot be blamed for the Yankees' slump. He was, however, at least partly responsible for his own bad season. First, he did not take care of himself during spring training in St. Petersburg. He stayed out too late, ate too much, and did not watch his diet, and when he began to feel ill he ignored it. The result was several weeks in the hospital and in bed at home, which meant out of baseball. Later on in the season he again started keeping late hours, showing up late for games. This time he was suspended for the better part of August, and fined $5000. Considering all those problems, a .290 average for the season was not bad at all.

The next year both Babe and the Yankees bounced back. Babe finished the season with a .372 average, which included 184 hits, 139 runs, two doubles, three triples, and 47 home runs. The Yankees won the American League pennant and just lost the World Series to the St. Louis Cardinals, 4 games to 3. Although the team was disappointed at not winning the Series, they were very proud of their comeback. They were also proud of Babe Ruth's comeback. At the end of the 1925 season, many sportswriters had solemnly stated that Babe was washed up. No one was saying that now.

Yankee manager "Hug" Huggins was perhaps proudest of all. He said to Ruth once:

"Babe, I admire a man who can win over a lot of tough opponents; but I admire even more a man who can win over himself."

"That's fine, Hug," Babe answered. "Do I get the fine back?"

"No," Hug answered.

"He wasn't a man who wasted words," Ruth later remarked about this exchange with his manager.

Looking back, the Yankees' 1926 season seems like just a warm-up for 1927. The 1927 Yankees were one of the greatest teams in baseball history. Every position was manned by a player who knew his game. The hitting strength alone was staggering. The club scored 975 runs altogether, and four men, Lazzeri, Meusel, Ruth, and

Gehrig, each batted in more than 100 runs. Two of them, Babe Ruth and Lou Gehrig, were in their second season as what would later prove to be one of the greatest batting duos of all time.

That season Gehrig topped Ruth, driving in 175 to Babe's 164. Babe scored 158 runs; Lou 149. They were the most powerful one-two punch the game had ever seen, with Babe batting third and Lou batting cleanup. From 1925 through 1934, when Ruth went to the Boston Braves, the two together hit a record 793 home runs.

In 1927 Lou Gehrig hit 47 homers. Babe Ruth hit 60! It was his highest home-run total yet, and it would prove to be the highest in his career. The newspaper sports headlines were full of the news, sixty home runs! And some had said the Babe was washed up after 1925!

Years later, Ruth would be modest about the record: "I don't think I ever would have established my home-run record of sixty if it hadn't been for Lou. . . . At one time we were almost neck and neck, and the papers were carrying what they called the home-run barometer showing what Lou and I were doing up to the minute. Pitchers began pitching to me, because if they passed me they still had Lou to contend with."

At the same time Babe would also be defensive about the record: "Speaking of my sixty home runs in nineteen twenty-seven, they were made before many of the parks had been artificially changed so as to favor the home-run hitter. I hit them into the same parks where, only a decade before, ten or twelve homers were good enough to win the title."

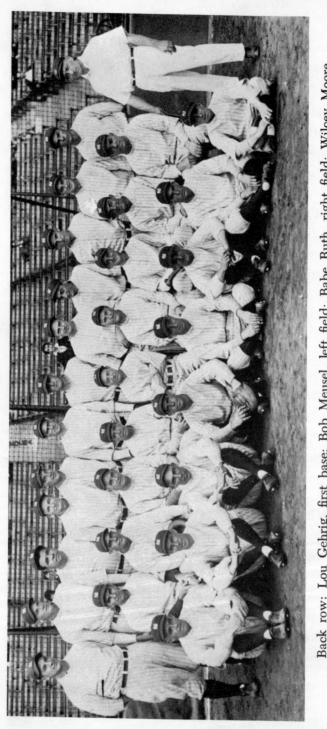

Back row: Lou Gehrig, first base; Bob Meusel, left field; Babe Ruth, right field; Wilcey Moore, pitcher; George Pipgras, pitcher; Earle Combs, center field; Miller; Waite Hoyt, pitcher; Tony Lazzeri, second base; Mark Koenig, shortstop; Urban Shocker, pitcher; Cedric Durst, outfield; Doc Woods, trainer. Center row: Bob Shawkey, pitcher; Joe Giard, pitcher; John Grabowski, catcher; Charlie O'Leary, coach; Miller Huggins, manager; Arthur Fletcher, coach; Herb Pennock, pitcher; Jules Wera, infield; Pat Collins, catcher. Front row: Walter (Dutch) Ruether, pitcher; Joe Dugan, third base: Ben Paschall, outfield; Benny Benbough, catcher; Myles Thomas, pitcher; Mike Gazella,

.The year that Babe Ruth hit his 500th career home run, the Yankees had supposedly the best team of all time. Here is the complete line-up of the 1927 New York Yankees.

(Private collection)

That is one argument that pro-Ruth baseball buffs would echo in 1973–1974, as Hank Aaron batted his way toward Babe's career home run record.

The 1927 season also saw Babe's 500th career home run. In fact, he finished the season with a career total of 517. While the total caused some stir in the baseball world, the reaction was not nearly as strong as it would be in later years, when other hitters passed the 500 mark. The reason is that in 1927 the baseball world was used to Babe Ruth breaking his own record. And it was used to Babe Ruth piling up homers. No one was even close to him in terms of career total. Only in later years would 500 be the important number it is today. And only today, when we know 714 is the magic number, do we see 500 as a home-run total that means the magic number 714 might be possible for a batter.

In 1963, at least in the spring, Hank Aaron was not thinking much about home-run totals. He was thinking about his average. Spring training that year was the worst of his career. He ended up with .206, with one home run and six runs batted in. While reporters and sportswriters began to forecast the end of Hank Aaron, Hank refused to feel pressured. After all, if he began to worry too much about his average at that point, his regular season average might be affected. He thought about his spring training average and tried to better his concentration, but he knew the average that counted would not be figured until the start of the regular season. If it was still bad then, it would be time to start worrying.

By April he was back in form, and he wound up the season with a .319 average. Had his average been just seven more percentage points, he would have won the National League Triple Crown. To win the Triple Crown, a batter must lead his league in batting average, in RBI's, and in home runs. Hank led the National League with 130 RBI's and tied Willie McCovey of the Giants for the home-run championship (each had 44). But the league-leading average was .326, and Hank's was only .319.

Hank was also rather proud of his 31 stolen bases. Not only was he Bad Henry with a bat, but he was Bad Henry on base as well. He was one of the best base-stealers in the league. He loved to catch the opposing infield off guard and slide in for a bonus base!

Nineteen sixty-three also saw the baseball world begin to take note of another important batting team. In the past, there had been duos like Babe Ruth and Lou Gehrig, Gil Hodges and Duke Snider of the Brooklyn Dodgers. Now there was Hank Aaron and Eddie Mathews. They had been teammates since 1954, and by the end of 1963, with Hank's 342 and Mathews' 350, together they had a total of 692 home runs.

Meanwhile rumors that the Braves would leave Milwaukee were rampant, and in 1964 the city's leaders began a campaign to keep the team. More fans went out to see the Braves that season than in any year since

1961, even though the team did little better than it had in 1963. At the end of the 1964 season the Braves announced that the team was moving to Atlanta after the 1965 season, and the fans ceased their support.

The Braves' home games in the season of 1965 were played to poor crowds and many empty seats. In a way it was a shame, for many Milwaukeeans missed their chance to see Hank Aaron and Eddie Mathews beat not only the home-run duo record of Gil Hodges and Duke Snider but also that of Babe Ruth and Lou Gehrig!

The Hodges-Snider record of 745 was broken on May 2 when Hank hit a long shot off Bo Belinsky of the Philadelphia Phillies in the second game of a doubleheader in Milwaukee. That brought his and Mathews' combined total of home runs hit as teammates to 746.

The two kept slugging away. By August 17 their total was 793, and on September 17 it reached 800. The baseball world had by this time begun to wonder if the Aaron-Mathews team had a chance at the Ruth-Gehrig record. Oddly enough, however, no one knew exactly what the latter record was. Everyone just assumed it was very high. After all, Ruth had wound up with a career home-run total of 714 and Gehrig with 494. When Aaron and Mathews reached 800, sportswriters and statisticians decided to figure out Ruth's and Gehrig's exact total.

To their surprise, they found that while Babe had hit many homers before Gehrig had made it to the Yankees and while Gehrig had continued to hit homers for the team after Babe went to Boston, they had only played together from 1925 through 1934. During that time they

Despite a broken ankle late in the 1954 season, Hank batted .280, hit 13 home runs, and was unanimous choice for the Braves' MVP. Here teammate Eddie Mathews rushes up to congratulate him after a score. Aaron and Mathews would later prove to be a record-breaking home run duo. *(United Press International)*

had hit, together, 793 homers. Aaron and Mathews had broken their record without anyone's even knowing it!

Neither Aaron nor Mathews let the feat go to his head. Hank, particularly, was so modest that his teammates showed more excitement than he did. By this time he and Mathews were the only two regulars on the team that had first brought baseball glory to Milwaukee, for pitcher Warren Spahn had been traded to the New York Mets earlier in the year. Yet they treated green rookies with a consideration that Hank, for one, had not known in his days as a rookie.

Asked what they thought of him, Hank's teammates always recalled times when they had first come to the club and Hank had helped them out or made them feel at home in some way. Most enthusiastic, perhaps, was Rico Carty. He had come to the Braves from the Dominican Republic early in 1964. Manager Bobby Bragan felt that Carty should room with someone who would help him learn English, and Hank volunteered. When Carty heard, through the interpreting of Felipe Alou, another Dominican on the team, that Hank Aaron had actually asked for him, he could not believe it. He never forgot how one of the stars on the team had made a scared kid in a strange country feel like an equal.

The Braves moved to Atlanta for the 1966 season, to the cheers of a whole new group of fans. And if the Braves did not exactly play championship ball, they played hard. No one played harder than Hank Aaron, who, by now, had deliberately become a pull hitter. He was aiming for the 500 home-run mark, although he never actually came out and said it. In that year he had 44 homers. In the next he had 37.

The year 1967 saw Hank reach a number of long-term records: he went beyond his 2,000th game, his 1,600th single, his 1,500th run, his 1,000th extra base hit, his 4,500th total base, his 2,600th hit, and his 1,500th RBI. But 1968 would be *the year* for Hank Aaron.

At the beginning of the regular 1968 season, Hank was enjoying one of the best starts of his career. He was hitting .350, had 12 RBI's and 6 homers by the end of April. Then he went into a slump. Then he broke out of the slump with two homers about a week later. Soon he went into another slump. Then he began to hit again. Then another slump. By July he was hitting again. By July 7 he had hit his 499th homer.

By July 14, even though the Braves had played a three-game series against the Dodgers, number 500 had not arrived. Herbert Aaron had gone to the Dodger games; perhaps over-eager to hit the 500th homer for his father, Hank had hit nothing but singles. By the time the Braves met the Giants on Sunday, July 14, Herbert Aaron had gone home to be with his wife.

"I was kind of disappointed that my father had to leave, although I understood why," Hank recalls. "While I always forget everything when a game starts and just concentrate on baseball, I wasn't feeling as 'up' as usual. Maybe the weather had something to do with it.

"There was thunder before the game, and as we started a few drops of rain began to fall. We kept on playing, though. My first time up, I hit a long drive into the left-field stands, and I thought maybe this was it. There wasn't a sound in the park. Everyone was watching that ball to see where it would go. Then, at the last minute, it curved foul. Back at the plate again, I grounded out.

"Then it really began to pour, and we had to stop the game for a good fifty minutes. We resumed play, with both teams scoreless at the end of the top of the third. We opened the bottom half of the third with Orlando Martinez up. He grounded out. Ron Reed, the pitcher, also grounded out. Then Felipe Alou hit a single, and Felix Millan hit another. We now had two outs and runners on first and second. Then it was my turn.

"The first two pitches Giants' pitcher Mike McCormick dealt up to me were outside. I fouled the next one into the stands, then let another ball pass. The count was now three and one.

"Then McCormick let go a beautiful fast ball. I guess he thought I'd let it go by and try for the walk. But I wanted that five hundred."

Hank hit that ball with a crack that could be heard throughout the stadium. The ball soared over the fence in left-center field, and this time there was no question about what it would do. Happily, Hank rounded the bases to a standing ovation from the crowd. Back at the plate, Alou, Millan, and Joe Torre greeted him. And then he was mobbed by the entire team.

While he was disappointed that his father had not seen the homer, Hank was excited about reaching the 500 mark. He was now the eighth man in baseball history to do so.

4/
Ruth and Aaron:
The Record

After passing the 500 home-run mark in 1927, Babe Ruth continued for six more years to wow the fans and other players alike with his batting prowess. In 1928 he hit 54 home runs and had a World Series batting average of .625, a record that was not broken for over 20 years. In 1929, although leg trouble allowed him to play in only 135 games, he batted .345, hit 46 homers, and batted in 154 runs. While the Yankees did not win the World Series that year, and thus missed the chance to claim four Series in a row, they could not complain about their gate receipts. Babe Ruth was still the biggest drawing card in baseball.

"Few ballplayers can point definitely to certain attendance figures and claim them as their own," Ruth later said. "It so happened that I could. Once, in Chicago, I came down sick and when it was announced in the papers two days before the scheduled appearance of the Yankees there on a Sunday, there were more than fifteen thousand cancellations of ticket orders."

Babe Ruth's following, of course, extended far beyond

the ball park. Every Yankee game was beamed over the air waves to the boxes in nearly everyone's living room—radios, the electronic wonders that had brought baseball, along with a lot of other things, into the home. Millions listened breathlessly to the play-by-play description of every game Babe Ruth was in. Others, older and perhaps suspicious of radio, continued to gather outside newspaper offices, watching the half-inning scores go up. Whatever their method of finding out, Americans *knew* about Babe Ruth. In fact, "What did the Babe do today?" was a question asked each day all over America. A candy bar, the Baby Ruth, was named after him. A song, " 'Batterin' Babe': Look at Him Now," became a national hit. In an era without TV, Babe Ruth was the best-known American of his time.

In 1930, although the Yankees finished third in the American League, Babe remained in top form, averaging .359 and hitting 49 homers. In 1931 his average was .373, the highest since 1924 when he won the batting championship. His 163 RBI total was the third highest of his career.

In 1932, Babe started "calling his homers," indicating before he hit the ball just where it would go. The Yankees were in Chicago, ready to play their third World Series game against the Cubs. The Yanks had already won the first two games in New York, and the Cubs fans had given them a terrible time upon their arrival in Chicago. Babe and his wife had actually been spat upon!

When Babe came up to bat, vegetables were hurled at him from the stands and the roaring boos of the crowd were deafening. Angry, Babe decided to show them a thing or two. Defiantly, he pointed to the top of the center-field bleachers. The crowd booed.

Cubs pitcher Root threw in two clean strike balls. After each strike, the crowd razzed Babe. But he wouldn't let them get to him. He called both strikes himself! He would later recall what happened next:

"Root threw me a fast ball. If I had let it go, it would have been called a strike. But this was *it*. I swung from the ground with everything I had, and as I hit the ball every muscle in my system, every sense I had, told me that I had never hit a better one, that as long as I lived nothing would ever feel as good as this.

"I didn't have to look up. But I did. That ball just went on and on and on and hit far up in the center-field bleachers in exactly the spot I had pointed to."

That home run was probably the most famous Babe ever hit, and it helped win the game for the Yankees, 7–5. They went on to win the World Series.

Nineteen thirty-one would prove to be the "top of the mountain" for Babe Ruth. In the next three seasons, while he hit 41, 34, and 22, homers respectively and maintained a good average, he missed many games. He was in his late thirties and he was tired.

By 1935 it was clear to him that the Yankees did not really want him any more. His salary, which had reached eighty thousand dollars in 1930, was now one dollar for the duration of spring training. He would have to prove himself before it was decided how much he would be paid. Babe realized the Yankees were in a bind. He had slowed up, especially in the field, but he was still sufficiently popular in New York to make the Yankee owner and manager afraid of the fans' reaction if they benched him or released him.

Babe solved the problem. He was too proud to work for one dollar and a "provisional contract." In the spring of 1935 he signed with the National League's Boston Braves.

But a new uniform did not make a new Babe. He was forty years old, and this was his twenty-second year in the big leagues. Everyone else, and, finally, Babe himself realized that that season was his last. On opening day in Boston, Babe hit a home run, but he was only batting .200 and really did not want to continue. He wanted to retire then, but he was persuaded to stay on through the Braves' first road trip.

"So I went west, for the last time," Babe later recalled, "and for one day in Pittsburgh I again was the old Babe Ruth. For one brief day I again wore the crown of the Sultan of Swat."

On that May afternoon Babe recovered for a brief instant the feel of earlier springs. With three swings, he hit homers 712, 713, and 714, and the last was the only ball that had ever been driven over the right-field roof at Pittsburgh's Forbes Field.

That was the last home run Babe Ruth would ever hit in his professional career. It did not break any records, except his own. He wasn't trying to pass anyone's mark —just play a little longer. His last team, the Boston Braves, was the forerunner of the Milwaukee Braves, the

This picture was taken only a few weeks before Babe, who had left the Yankees and joined the Boston Red Sox, announced his retirement from baseball. He would go on one more road trip, with Boston, and in one game would hit home runs number 712, 713, and 714. *(Wide World Photos)*

team on which Hank Aaron would begin to play nineteen years later.

Babe did not want to leave baseball. For several years he went to St. Petersburg, Florida, in the spring and watched Yankee exhibition games from the stands. He went to regular season games as well. Once in a while, he would be called upon to stand up and wave, and the crowds would applaud, remembering the Babe of earlier days. He died fourteen years later, in 1948, and the world—not just the baseball world but the whole world—mourned his passing. Everything about him, from his body to his grin to his talent to his appetite for pleasure and fame to his love for baseball, had been big. He was a monumental figure, a sports legend. There would never be another Babe.

In 1968 the country began to take note of Hank Aaron. He had been known in the baseball world for many years, but except for times when he approached records, the general public had been largely unaware of him. In fact, Hank Aaron is perhaps the most "un-star-like" star in the history of baseball.

For years he had been known as "the best all-around ballplayer in baseball history." That is the kind of accolade that a baseball writer or real baseball buff appreciates, but the general public, the average fan, does not. Hank, for one, feels the publicity he is getting now is long overdue.

"After all," he said in 1973, "I haven't just started hitting home runs. I've been hitting home runs for nineteen years. Only now I am getting the kind of publicity that other ballplayers were getting ten to fifteen years ago."

Yet Hank would never have wanted, or sought, publicity for other reasons than plain good ballplaying. He realizes that many other "stars" have been both baseball players and performers. That kind of stardom has never been his desire.

"I don't want to be thought of as anything but a good ballplayer," he has often said. "I was never a 'Say Hey' kid, I was never a Mickey Mantle or a Roger Maris [of the 1961 Yankees]. I was never a showman. I have always played the best I could in the best way I could."

It has always been the same off the field in his private life. While Babe Ruth traveled with his "fair-weather friends," as he called them, staying in expensive hotel suites while the rest of his team rented inexpensive rooms in less pretentious hotels, Hank Aaron always stayed where the team stayed. While Babe Ruth drove a fancy roadster, Hank Aaron drove a Chevrolet Caprice. Babe Ruth smoked big cigars, drank quantities of booze, dressed nattily, spent his nights on the town, spent money thoughtlessly, played the celebrity role to the hilt. Hank Aaron does not smoke, drinks moderately, dresses well but not flashily, spends as much time as he can with his family and rarely on the town, doesn't throw money around, and behaves in such an average manner that sportswriters have been known to throw up their hands in despair over the problem of writing interesting copy about him. A writer can cover the "just an average guy" angle so many times before it becomes boring.

Hank could not help his lack of showmanship. In a way, it was inherited. Mr. and Mrs. Herbert Aaron had refused, for example, their son's offer of a new home. "We're happy here," Stella Aaron says. "We bought this house on Edwards Street ourselves, we like the neighborhood. Why should we move?" Hank Aaron is lucky to have parents like that. Babe Ruth was not.

During his 1968 season, when he hit his 500th home run and finished with 29 for a career total of 504, Hank Aaron was in every newspaper and magazine, and on most television and radio stations. If his name was not on "everybody's lips," it was certainly on the lips of those who knew baseball. Hank had a fairly good season in 1969, hitting for a .300 average. His 44 home runs that season were 15 more than his 1968 total. He was clearly concentrating on hitting home runs now. The Braves had a good season, too, one of the best in years. They made it all the way to the National League Championship play-offs, but they lost the series to the New York Mets.

In 1970 Hank again made headlines when, on Sunday, May 17, he got the 3000th hit of his career against the Reds at Cincinnati's Crowley Field. It was an infield dribbler that was almost fielded by Cincinnati. But just in case anyone thought that was a lousy 3000th hit, Hank's 3001st was a home run over the left-field fence. Stan Musial, the most recent 3000-hitter at that time, was on hand for the game; his 3001st hit had also been a homer. Hank finished the season with a .298 average and 38 home runs.

Yankee great Roger Maris commented later: "Henry could steal fifty bases a year if he wanted to and seldom get caught, but he knows that he might get hurt, and that would harm his ball club in the long run. In some ways it is unfortunate that Henry's hitting is so outstanding. It tends to overshadow his other talents."

Nineteen seventy-one would prove to be Hank's greatest season until then. On the night of April 27 he became only the third player in history to hit 600 career home runs. He also led his team in home runs, with 47. In 1972 his average, and his home run total, dropped—.265, 34 homers. Yet by then his career totals were so high that long-term hitting records had little chance to stand. He tied the all-time National League grand slam homer mark when he hit the 14th of his career. With his 649th career home run, he passed Willie Mays' record to become second on the all-time homer list.

Then, in 1973, it all broke open. Hank started the season with 673 home runs. Babe Ruth's record was clearly within reach. Suddenly, all eyes were on Hank Aaron again.

A popular song was written, entitled "Move Over Babe, Here Comes Henry." It sold very well.

He was besieged by reporters asking questions, questions, questions. He did not mind, usually; he enjoyed the well-earned limelight. But his years of near anonymity haunted him still.

A twenty-two-year-old New York secretary, knowing a young man she admired was a sports fan, invited him to her apartment to watch one of the 1973 World Series games between the New York Mets and the Baltimore Orioles. The national anthem was played and the teams ran out on the field to start the game. Excitedly, the girl asked, "Which one's Hank Aaron?" Her boy friend stared at her in disbelief.

Hank has his own anecdotes.

"One time, during the All-Star game," he recalls, "this reporter came up to me. He was all praise and flattery, said he'd been following my career for nearly twenty years. Then he asked me, 'Which do you hit—left or right?' Can you imagine that?"

Then there were the letters, the majority good, wishing him luck. One of Hank's favorites was from a young boy who wrote, "I only eat 'Oh Henry!' candy bars." A sizable minority, however, were not fit to read.

Hank tried very hard to take it all in stride, not to let the pressure get to him. He finished the 1973 season with 40 homers for a career total of 713, just one short of Babe Ruth's career total, a record that had stood unchallenged for nearly 40 years. In a way, Hank was relieved. Certainly he would like to have hit 714 by the end of 1973. But he had not, and the pressure was off for the winter—or so he thought.

The pressure continued. The public had been awakened to Hank Aaron, the challenger for Babe Ruth's record, and the media aimed to *keep* the public awake this time. There were television programs on his career, pages and pages of magazines told his story, at least five books on his career were scheduled for publication in the spring and summer of 1974. Contests were announced: Pick the day when Aaron hits number 714 and you win a——. Hank Aaron . . . Hank Aaron . . . Hank Aaron. The name echoed across the country, and all eyes turned to the beginning of the 1974 season. It was no longer a question of "if"; it was only a question of "when."

For his part, Hank finally started to do a little capitalizing on his fame. He signed contracts to endorse products; he collaborated on books about his life, for a fee or a share of the royalties. But these were matters of money. He capitalized on the human side as well.

Twenty years earlier, as a young black ballplayer in a nearly all-white league, he had determined that someday he would speak out on racial matters, someday when he had achieved his early goals and become a champion and would be listened to. Now, in 1973–1974, he did.

"When you're speaking your piece, and it doesn't go anywhere, then you just wait until the right time," he says. "When I had four to five hundred home runs, nobody listened to Henry Aaron. So I felt, I'm just going to wait. When I begin to challenge Ruth's record, then everybody will want to listen and see what Henry Aaron has to say." Like Kareem Abdul Jabbar and Bill Russell of basketball, Hank waited until people wanted to listen to him, and then he spoke his piece.

He made public some of the hate mail he was receiving —not to get sympathy, but to remind white America that it still had a lot to learn in the area of humanity. He used the letters, too, to illustrate to young blacks the need for determination in "making it" in predominantly white society. During the summer of 1973 Hank was a guest of the Chicago Little League. He read one of the hate letters he had recently received, a "nigger" letter. When he finished he told the young audience, "Things like this just make me push that much harder. As a young player in Mobile, Alabama, I realized that being a black person, I already had two strikes against me, and I certainly wasn't going to let them get the third strike. Being a black baseball player, I only had one way to go, and that was up."

He also began to work with Reverend Jesse L. Jackson, of Operation PUSH, a black self-help organization. He spoke of what it was like to be a black man in America.

The hate mail really did not bother him that much. As a black man born and reared in the South, he had dealt with being called a "nigger" long before. He realized that while some of the writers of those letters truly did not want to see a black man beat a white man's record, others simply did not want to see "The Babe" bested by anyone, white or black. He happened to be black, and the obvious epithet for him was "nigger." If he had been white, it could have been "wop" or "guinea" or "kike."

What bothered Hank more were what he considered the more subtle forms of racism. Quietly, with an obvious trace of bitterness, he tells of the time in 1968 when, after he had hit 500 home runs, his bat and the baseball were sent to the Baseball Hall of Fame at Cooperstown, New York. The Hall of Fame did not even acknowledge receiving them. He tells of hitting his 700th homer and not receiving a word of congratulation from baseball commissioner Bowie Kuhn.

"I think that if I'd been white I probably would have

When Hank hit his 700th homer in 1973, it was the prelude to baseball history. Would he break Babe Ruth's home run record, which had stood for nearly 40 years? *(Atlanta Braves)*

After hitting his 700th homer, Hank ran the bases as easily as he had for his other home runs, but from that point on great pressure was put upon him. *(Atlanta Braves)*

gotten a telegram from the commissioner," Hank says. "A lot of people say this is a small thing to keep on talking about. Well, I don't think it's small, really. I understand his position. As he explained to me, if he started sending telegrams out, he would be sending them to everybody who hit four doubles, three home runs. My answer to him was that it's probably going to be a long, long time before he's going to see anybody hit seven hundred home runs, and I didn't think one telegram would hurt. I still feel that way about it."

Despite such instances of what he regarded as subtle racism, despite the hate mail, despite the long, long time it had taken America to take note of him, Hank Aaron was finally receiving the attention he deserved, and he was enjoying it. In the 1974 season he would hit 715 home runs, and then some. He would break Babe Ruth's long-standing record and set one of his own. And then, at the end of the season, he would retire, assured of his own important place in baseball history. He would be forty years old, the same age as Babe Ruth when he retired.

The 1974 baseball season officially opened on April 4, and for the Atlanta Braves it opened in Cincinnati, Ohio. Fifty-one thousand fans were on hand to watch Hank Aaron, among them baseball commissioner Bowie Kuhn and Vice President Gerald Ford. Earlier, there had been some controversy over whether Hank would play in the opening series at Cincinnati. The Braves wanted to make sure he would hit homer number 714 in Atlanta, and tried to keep him out of the games at Cincinnati. Commissioner Bowie Kuhn had ruled that he must play, and so, in the first inning of the game, Hank Aaron walked to the plate for his first time at bat.

Two men were on base and there was one out. Jack Billingham, the Reds' pitcher, was nervous. He realized that if he was not careful, he would go down in history as "the man who pitched Hank's 714th." He was low on the first pitch, then missed the plate with a slow curve for ball two. Hank took a fast ball for a strike, then the count went to three balls and one strike on a low outside sinker.

"The ball was slippery," Billingham told a New York Times reporter. "On the next pitch, I threw a sinker. It was going toward the outside part of the plate and it tailed in. It was my mistake. But that's what makes Hank Aaron great. He hits mistakes."

"Billingham threw me a fast ball and I was guessing fast ball," said Hank. The 400-foot three-run line drive went over a fence in left center field. Hammerin' Hank had matched Babe Ruth's record exactly six minutes into the 1974 season!

The game was held up another six minutes while Hank received ovation after ovation from the crowd. Commissioner Kuhn made a speech congratulating him. Vice President Ford did, too. For his part, Hank's words were brief. After the usual thank-you, he said simply, "I'm just glad it's almost over with."

One thing pleased him very much. His father, who had gone home to be with his wife the day before Hank had hit his 500th homer, was there to see him hit his 714th. After the speeches, Hank had walked over to the box where his father and older brother, Herbert Jr., were sitting. "I was just so happy they were there to see this home run," he said.

Hank went hitless in the third and final game at Cincinnati. Some outsiders charged that he was deliberately saving home run number 715 for the home crowd in Atlanta. Those who really knew Hank, however, scoffed at the charge. The sportswriters and other baseball players knew that Hank gave each game everything he had. That was the only way he knew how to play.

On Monday April 8, 1974, the Braves met the Los Angeles Dodgers for their first home game of the season in Atlanta Stadium, and if there had been pressure on Hank before, it was nothing compared to the pressure on

Exactly six minutes into the 1974 season, Hank hit homer number 714 to tie Babe Ruth's record. He hit it in Cincinnati against the Reds. The Braves had wanted him to hit number 714 at home in Atlanta, but Hank could not hold back.

(United Press International)

him now. Atlanta had prepared a grand tribute to their star, perhaps the most lavish ceremony ever in the history of baseball. Figures from Hank's past—his parents, Ed Scott, the man who had first signed him to the Mobile Bears, Charley Grimm, his first Braves manager, Donald Davidson, the Braves' traveling secretary who first called Henry "Hammerin' Hank," and many others—spoke of their memories of Hank in a kind of "This Is Your Life" presentation. Dignitaries like Atlanta's Mayor Maynard Jackson and Congressman Andrew Young praised him. Singer-star Sammy Davis, Jr., promised a large donation to the "Hank Aaron Scholarship Fund." Still another song about him was played over the public address system: "Hey, Hank, I know you're gonna do it, but please don't hit it offa me. The Babe's up there watchin' you and pullin' for you . . ."

A bronze bust of Hank was unveiled. It portrayed him smiling, which is his usual expression. A frequent comment about Hank by sportswriters is, "He smiles about as easily as anyone I've ever seen."

In the face of all these honors, the man who smiles so easily showed that he could shed a few tears of happiness as well. Hank had been waiting a long time for all this.

The pressure, however, must have been almost unbearable. Behind all the celebration, there was tension. If Hank did not hit home run number 715 that day, the ceremonies would have a slightly hollow ring. It was a "show of shows," and it needed that homer to be complete. Hank realized this and said, "I just hope I can hit that homer for the folks tonight."

Finally the game began, and so did a light drizzle. The stands were dotted with umbrellas. His first time up, Hank was walked by Los Angeles pitcher Al Downing. The crowd booed. They had not come to the stadium to sit in the rain and watch their star go to first base on four balls. Henry scored in that inning, reaching home on a double play, and even made a little history doing that. It was the 2063rd time he had crossed home plate in the majors, breaking the National League record held by Willie Mays and placing him behind American Leaguers Ty Cobb and Babe Ruth.

By the fourth inning the rain still had not stopped, and the air was chilly and raw. The score was 3–1 in favor of the Dodgers, and the Braves were up. Lead-off batter Darrel Evans reached first base on an error, and then the crowd began to cheer. Hank Aaron strolled to the batter's box and, wearing his usual number, 44, faced Al Downing, who also wore number 44.

Downing's first pitch hit the dirt. Once more the crowd booed. Then came the second pitch, and Hank took his first swing of the night. The crack of the bat as it hit the ball was "heard round the world." The ball rose high toward left center, and the crowd came to its feet, shouting, watching. Hank Aaron saw the ball drop over the inside fence separating the outfield from the bull pen area. He broke his stride and began to trot. At the same time he sort of shook his head, as if to say, "Thank God it's all over with."

In the ceremonies that followed, that is exactly what he did say, and little else. His 715th homer had broken

Babe Ruth's record and had broken the intense pressure that had been on Hank for nearly a year. From then on he would just be breaking his own record in regular season home runs.

In regular season plus All Star and World Series games, Babe Ruth's career total was 730. On June 5, 1974, in the seventh inning of a game against the Phillies, Hank hit a grand-slam homer. It was the sixteenth of his career and gave him the National League record for grand-slams. It was the 723rd homer of his career in regular season games. Counting World Series and All

The Braves' first home game in the 1974 season was marked by great ceremony in Henry Aaron's honor. His second time at bat, Hank broke Babe Ruth's home run record with number 715.

(United Press International)

Star games, it was his 731st homer, breaking yet another record of Babe Ruth's.

Meanwhile the controversy over the record continues and will continue for years to come. It is a controversy with many aspects. The two major aspects, perhaps, are the color bar and the generation gap.

Racism plays a larger role in the controversy than many Americans would like to admit. Just as the boxing match between Joe Louis and Max Schmeling in 1938 was seen as a battle between black and white, so Hank Aaron's approach toward Babe Ruth's record was seen by many as an assault upon white supremacy in baseball. Today, of course, it is not fashionable to admit to racism, and so those who refuse to accept the breaking of Babe Ruth's record by a black man cite statistics and historical reasons why the Babe's record should stand.

The generation gap is also an important part of the controversy. While nearly every young sandlot slugger has heard of Babe Ruth, very few know much about him. After all, he has been dead over twenty-five years, and by 1974 nearly forty years had passed since he hit his 714th home run. Most young people rely on their fathers and grandfathers to tell them about Babe Ruth's career and about how the name Babe Ruth was once on nearly everyone's lips nearly every day.

For their part, many of the fathers and grandfathers look back to the days of Babe Ruth and their own youth as the "good old days." Hank Aaron is nothing like the Babe, they say.

Hank Aaron has noticed this difference in generations.

"Most of the young fans understand what I'm going through," he says, "and one reason is that they want to relate to a ballplayer of their time. They want to be able to say, 'I saw Henry Aaron play.' 'I saw Henry Aaron when he hit seven hundred.' 'I saw Henry Aaron when he hit seven hundred and fourteen.' They don't know a thing about Babe Ruth. They know something about Henry Aaron.

"The grown-ups want to live in the past. They want to think about the time when they saw Babe Ruth forty years ago. They don't want his mark erased. They want his mark to stand."

Arguments based on "Babe is the best because I saw him play" or "Hank is the best because I saw him play" are not very good either. So both the younger generation and the older generation also cite statistics and historical reasons why their man deserves the record.

The statistics and historical reasons why one or the other man should be the true Home Run King abound. Babe Ruth had to hit most of his homers with a non-tapered bat, and the ball was a mush bag compared to that of today, say the pro-Ruth people. On the other hand, Babe Ruth never had to play night ball. Night ball, with those artificial lights and the eye strain they give you, can take a couple of years off a player's career, the pro-Aaron people say. Ruth was really the better hitter, say the pro-Ruth people: his lifetime batting average was .342, Aaron's is just over .300. The pro-Aaron people retort that Ruth never got 3000 hits; Hank Aaron has.

"You have been to bat 2700 more times than Babe Ruth," one letter Hank received in the summer of 1973 said, before it went into the "nigger" refrain. "If Babe Ruth was at bat 2700 more times, he would have hit 814 home runs." Other pro-Ruth people agree with the importance of this statistic. Seasons are longer now than they were in Ruth's time, they say, and, anyway, Ruth started out as a pitcher, playing and hitting only once every three or four games. Actually, Hank hit his 714th homer on his 11,289th major league time at bat, compared with 8,399 for Babe Ruth. However, as Aaron fans are quick to point out, Hank played with the Indianapolis Clowns and with the Braves' minor league teams at Eau Claire and Jacksonville for two years before he made the major leagues. The Clowns' statistics are lost at this point, but with the two Milwaukee minor teams Hank hit 31 homers. If all the home runs he hit in those two years counted, he would have passed Babe's record long before he did. Babe only played part of a season before he made the majors, and hit only one homer during that time. Anyway, in Babe's time balls that bounced over or through fences were counted as homers, and no records were kept on those balls.

Players today have to play many more exhibition games, in which home runs do not count toward career totals. This pressure to start playing too early each year saps a player's strength.

Pitchers were more formidable in Ruth's time, at least in the beginning, because they were allowed to throw trick balls. Aaron could not have hit against them as well as Ruth did.

Many ball parks are larger today than in Ruth's time. If Aaron had had to play in them, he would not have hit so many homers. But Ruth, unlike Aaron, never had to suffer jet lag after transcontinental flights. Coast-to-coast league franchises have added more than 20,000 miles to every team's travel schedule. The physical strain makes it impossible for even a superstar to be "up" at all times.

The arguments, pro and con, go on and on. Most contain some logic, but in an emotionally charged situation like the breaking of Babe Ruth's record there are always some arguments that make no sense at all. A comical example is the pro-Ruth argument that the air in Atlanta is lighter than New York air, enabling the batter to drive a ball out of the Braves' stadium even when he gets only a piece of it. Needless to say, no one who uses this argument ever mentions who weighed the air!

The fact is, none of these arguments is decisive. Two baseball players can only be compared, rightly, if they have played under the same conditions, in the same parks, in the same era. The era and conditions under which Babe Ruth hit his 714 homers are as different from the era and conditions under which Hank Aaron hit his as Babe Ruth, the man, was different from Hank Aaron, the man.

Babe Ruth played in the high noon of baseball, when it was the "American pastime." He was part of the legendary Yankee dynasty, the winningest team in major league history. Hank Aaron has played in a time when professional football and basketball have stolen much of baseball's excitement. His team has not won a World Series since 1958; it is hardly a dynasty.

When Babe Ruth began to play baseball, the game was one for big, burly men with strange nicknames who were willing to swelter in the hot sun in woolen suits, on unkempt fields where the blue sky came down to meet the green grass. The country abounded with minor leagues, and small-town fame was the most the average player could expect. He could also expect to play a long, long time and make little money. Americans who could not go to the ball park had to wait outside the newspaper office to see half-inning scores, or read about their favorite teams the next day or the next week. Bats were slimmer, balls were fatter, gloves were smaller. The pitcher was supreme. Any trick ball he could think of was legal, and ball parks were not designed for home runs.

Babe Ruth, almost singlehandedly, began a revolution in baseball. His early fantastic home-run totals caused America to get home-run fever, and the world of baseball quickly caught it too. Equipment, fields, rules were changed to increase the possibility of home runs. The scale tipped from the side of the pitcher to the side of the hitter.

Meanwhile, the radio found its way into nearly every home, and with it came baseball. It became the national pastime and Babe Ruth became a national idol.

Even in Ruth's final season, baseball was far different from the game Hank Aaron was to play. The first night game was played in May 1935, the same month Ruth played his last game. It happened at Crosley Field in Cincinnati, Ohio. Sportswriters reported that the game became a strangely colorless, artificial event. Players complained that they were afraid to dig in at the plate, afraid that they would not see the ball, afraid of being hit by the ball. The fans complained that they were cold and could not see the players very well. No one thought night baseball would ever last.

Night baseball did last, and today it is a fact of the game, along with transcontinental airplane flights that enable a New York team to play a California team one day and an Atlanta team two days later. Gloves are bigger, bats are better. Uniforms are now made of comfortable synthetic fibers. Television beams games across the country, and threatens gate receipts at the parks. Home games, in fact, are often blacked out on local television. The scale has tipped back to the side of the pitcher. Babe Ruth tipped it the other way, but after twenty-five years or so, around 1950, it began to tip back. Today, baseball is a pitcher's game. Hits are kept to a minimum; the no-hitter is the biggest story in baseball now.

Baseball will continue to change in the years to come. No one really knows how. One thing that seems to be evident: it will be some time before there is another Henry Aaron or Willie Mays. Changes in the game do not favor high career home run totals for young hitters like Johnny Bench. In 1971, after playing four years, Bench was behind both Aaron and Mays in their first four years by 23 to 29 homers, 35 to 216 hits, 2 to 67 RBI's and 32 to 40 points. The reason is not so much talent as it is fifteen years and a few thousand more games played on mostly synthetic fields against tough pitchers and many more thousands of miles of road games between him and them. Still, maybe someday the scale will be tipped back in favor of the hitter and a player will hit 900 or 1000 home runs in his career. Maybe someday a team on the field will make a clean triple play. Will that batter in the future, then, be compared to Hank Aaron or Babe Ruth? Will that fielder be compared to other great fielders?

In their excitement over Hank Aaron's challenge to Babe Ruth's record, many forget that there is one way in which Babe Ruth and Hank Aaron are very much the same. It is a similarity that should always be remembered. Both men played baseball in the tradition of true sportsmen—fairly, courageously, and with a sheer love of the game and a talent that make a true baseball great.

The two share another similarity, and while the controversy rages, perhaps it would be well for us to remember it. Babe Ruth would not have wanted, and Hank Aaron does not want, his record to stand forever.

"If Babe were alive today," says Mrs. Babe Ruth, "he would be cheering Hank Aaron on. Hank Aaron is setting a record of his own, for someone else to shoot at."

Perhaps Hank Aaron expresses best the way we all should feel about the home run record, or any record, for that matter: "I believe that records are made to be broken, and I just hope that ten years or fifteen years from now some kid will come along and challenge my record, and whether he is black or white, I certainly will be pulling for him."

BABE RUTH'S BATTING RECORD

Age	Year	Club	League	Games	At Bat
19	1914	Balt.-Prov.	Int.	46	121
*					
19	1914	Boston	A.L.	5	10
20	1915	Boston	A.L.	42	92
21	1916	Boston	A.L.	67	136
22	1917	Boston	A.L.	52	123
23	1918	Boston	A.L.	95	317
24	1919	Boston	A.L.	130	432
25	1920	New York	A.L.	142	458
26	1921	New York	A.L.	152	540
27	1922	New York	A.L.	110	403
28	1923	New York	A.L.	152	522
29	1924	New York	A.L.	153	529
30	1925	New York	A.L.	98	359
31	1926	New York	A.L.	152	495
32	1927	New York	A.L.	151	540
33	1928	New York	A.L.	154	536
34	1929	New York	A.L.	135	499
35	1930	New York	A.L.	145	518
36	1931	New York	A.L.	145	534
37	1932	New York	A.L.	133	457
38	1933	New York	A.L.	137	459
39	1934	New York	A.L.	125	365
40	1935	Boston	N.L.	28	72
Major League Totals				2503	8396

* Beginning of Major League career

HANK AARON'S BATTING RECORD

Age	Year	Club	League	Games	At Bat
18	1952	Eau Claire	North.	87	345
19 *	1953	Jacksonville	So. Atl.	137	574
20	1954	Milwaukee	N.L.	122	468
21	1955	Milwaukee	N.L.	153	602
22	1956	Milwaukee	N.L.	153	609
23	1957	Milwaukee	N.L.	151	615
24	1958	Milwaukee	N.L.	153	601
25	1959	Milwaukee	N.L.	154	629
26	1960	Milwaukee	N.L.	153	590
27	1961	Milwaukee	N.L.	155	603
28	1962	Milwaukee	N.L.	156	592
29	1963	Milwaukee	N.L.	161	631
30	1964	Milwaukee	N.L.	145	570
31	1965	Milwaukee	N.L.	150	570
32	1966	Atlanta	N.L.	158	603
33	1967	Atlanta	N.L.	155	600
34	1968	Atlanta	N.L.	160	606
35	1969	Atlanta	N.L.	147	547
36	1970	Atlanta	N.L.	150	516
37	1971	Atlanta	N.L.	139	495
38	1972	Atlanta	N.L.	129	449
39	1973	Atlanta	N.L.	120	392
40	1974	Atlanta	N.L.		
Major League Totals				2964	11288

* Beginning of Major League career

BABE RUTH'S BATTING RECORD

Runs	Hits	Doubles	Triples	Home Runs	Runs Batted in	Batting Average
22	28	2	10	1	...	.231
1	2	1	0	0	0	.200
16	29	10	1	4	20	.315
18	37	5	3	3	16	.272
14	40	6	3	2	10	.325
50	95	26	11	11	64	.300
103	139	34	12	29	112	.322
158	172	36	9	54	137	.376
177	204	44	16	59	170	.378
94	128	24	8	35	96	.315
151	205	45	13	41	130	.393
143	200	39	7	46	121	.378
61	104	12	2	25	66	.290
139	184	30	5	47	155	.372
158	192	29	8	60	164	.356
163	173	29	8	54	142	.323
121	172	26	6	46	154	.345
150	186	28	9	49	153	.359
149	199	31	3	46	163	.373
120	156	13	5	41	137	.341
97	138	21	3	34	103	.301
78	105	17	4	22	84	.288
13	13	0	0	6	12	.181
2174	2873	506	136	714	2209	.342

HANK AARON'S BATTING RECORD

Runs	Hits	Doubles	Triples	Home Runs	Runs Batted in	Batting Average
79	116	19	4	9	61	.336
115	208	36	14	22	125	.362
58	131	27	6	13	69	.280
105	189	37	9	27	106	.314
106	200	34	14	26	92	.328
118	198	27	6	44	132	.322
109	196	34	4	30	95	.326
116	223	46	7	39	123	.355
102	172	20	11	40	126	.292
115	197	39	10	34	120	.327
127	191	28	6	45	128	.323
121	201	29	4	44	130	.319
103	187	30	2	24	95	.328
109	181	40	1	32	89	.318
117	168	23	1	44	127	.279
113	184	37	3	39	109	.307
84	174	33	4	29	86	.287
100	164	30	3	44	97	.300
103	154	26	1	38	118	.298
95	162	22	3	47	118	.327
75	119	10	0	34	77	.265
84	118	12	1	40	96	.301
2060	3509	584	96	713	2133	.310

MILESTONE HOME RUNS

No.			*For*	*Against*
1	Ruth	May 6, 1915	Red Sox	Yankees
	Aaron	April 23, 1954	Milwaukee Braves	Cardinals
50	Ruth	May 1, 1920	Yankees	Red Sox
	Aaron	July 6, 1956	Milwaukee Braves	Cubs
100	Ruth	Sept. 24, 1920	Yankees	Senators
	Aaron	August 15, 1957	Milwaukee Braves	Reds
200	Ruth	May 12, 1923	Yankees	Tigers
	Aaron	July 3, 1960	Milwaukee Braves	Cardinals
300	Ruth	Sept. 8, 1925	Yankees	Red Sox
	Aaron	April 19, 1963	Milwaukee Braves	Mets
400	Ruth	Sept. 2, 1927	Yankees	Athletics
	Aaron	April 20, 1966	Atlanta Braves	Phillies
500	Ruth	August 11, 1929	Yankees	Indians
	Aaron	July 26, 1968	Atlanta Braves	Giants
600	Ruth	August 21, 1931	Yankees	Browns
	Aaron	April 27, 1971	Atlanta Braves	Giants
700	Ruth	July 13, 1934	Yankees	Tigers
	Aaron	July 21, 1973	Atlanta Braves	Phillies
714	Ruth	May 25, 1935	Boston Braves	Pirates
	Aaron	April 4, 1974	Atlanta Braves	Reds
715	Aaron	April 8, 1974	Atlanta Braves	Dodgers